BEYOND YOUR INBOX: INTENTIONAL LEADERSHIP IN A DISTRACTED WORLD

MELISSA CREEDE

Published by
Hybrid Global Publishing
333 E 14th Street
#3C
New York, NY 10003

Manufactured in the United States of America, or in the United Kingdom when distributed elsewhere.

Creede, Melissa
Beyond Your Inbox: Intentional Leadership in a Distracted World
    ISBN: 978-1-961757-54-7
    eBook: 978-1-961757-55-4
    LCCN: requested

Cover design by: Natasha Clawson
Copyediting by: Sue Toth
Interior design by: Suba Murugan
Author photo by: Bill Juillette

DISCLAIMER

WEBSITE

DEDICATION

To all those who create transformational change within
themselves and others to make the world better,
even when it's uncomfortable, especially
when it's uncomfortable.

ACKNOWLEDGEMENTS

"I don't think I could do this alone. I don't think I want to."
— Scully, The X-Files

I have many people to thank not just for helping me birth this book, but also for making me the person and the leader that I am today.

My amazing daughters Maya and Micaella, who every single day hold up a metaphorical mirror for me to see myself in: my strengths, my areas for growth, my hopes, my fears, and most of all my deepest desires for the future of the planet and of a just and loving world. Being a mom to you both is an honour, a privilege, and an incredible learning and growth experience. You continue to amaze and inspire me.

For my husband Maurizio, for being a stable and solid presence through inevitable ups and downs that life throws us, and for giving me the space and freedom to be myself and to pursue whatever crazy experiences call my attention.

To my sister Cate, who pushes me to think bigger and never be complacent with the status quo. I am so thankful to have you in my life. I am a better human because of you. You continuously challenge me to grow, to reflect deeply, to grapple with my place and my role in the world around me. *"Dear god, this parachute is a knapsack."* — Friends

Mom, thank you for always being there for me and for modeling a beautiful, generous spirit rooted in service and a desire to help and teach others. You ignited my independence and grit. Dad, your intellectual wonder and eccentricity flows through me. I wish to thank you both, mom and dad, and my family for instilling this deep curiosity and love for learning in me. I've taken it all to heart.

My extended family – in all your weird and wacky ways, you have also shaped who I am.

To my Orioles Flock, who embarked with me on my personal transformational leadership journey and to my Platypus Puddle who propelled me to even grander aspirations.

The countless and varied coaches, mentors, guides, and healers in my own leadership journey – there are far, far too many of you to name, but every single one of you has shaped me into the person and the leader that I am today, and you will forever be a part of me as I continue to evolve!

And lastly, to Shari, thank you for hearing my voice, my ideas, and my vision, and seamlessly partnering to get all of this into written and book form. You are a joy to work with!

CONTENTS

CHAPTER 1

What Does Success Look Like? Strategic Habits from a Leadership Coach

"Most of the time change is a good thing and I think that's what it's all about—embracing change, being brave, doing whatever you have to so everyone in your life can move forward with theirs. You say impossible, but all I hear is 'I'm possible.'"

— *Ted Lasso*

I've coached leaders and changemakers for 15 years, and I've had many clients who are told they should be more strategic, but they don't really know what this means or how to do this. Most people think being more strategic means something formal like writing a strategic plan. While that is a useful exercise that forces us to think and plan more strategically, there is so much more to it than that.

This, essentially, is a how-to book.

If you are a leader or an up-and-coming leader who wants to lead more effectively (lead people, lead projects, lead towards a vision, or lead transformative change in your organization, your community or in the world), and you want to be more strategic and intentional about where you're heading, if you want to be invited to higher level meetings, if you want to be considered for higher level projects and roles, or if you want to work on complex systemic social change but you get derailed by day-to-day demands, then this book is for you.

When I share with my clients what I've learned about leadership and being more strategic, they often ask to be directed to a resource to learn more about these techniques. And while there are many great leadership books out there – and I encourage you to be a lifelong learner of leadership if you want to lead – I have not found a resource that outlines what I'm sharing. This is what drove me to put these concepts into a book.

A big part of being more strategic is what you deliberately pay attention to and focus on in terms of your time, what you think about, the questions you ask yourself and others, how you show up, and of course what you actually do.

Because asking good, strategic questions is a skill to be learned and refined, I've bolded questions throughout the book to help you recognize and practice them. These might be questions you ask others, or they might be questions you ask yourself. It doesn't matter if you don't know the answers. In fact, often you likely won't know the answers right away – that's probably a good indication that you're asking the right questions. The questions help you think, they help you imagine a different state, understand a different viewpoint, expand your mind, help you be curious and adaptive.

My favourite question of all — "What does success look like?" — is the inspiration for this book. It can be used in any circumstance really from defining a vision two, five, and ten years into the future to defining how you want a specific conversation in the moment or meeting to play out, or how you want to come across in a presentation—really anything at all.

The approaches, habits, and tools I share in this book have been proven and endorsed by the thousands of leaders that I've coached over the years. Good luck in your own leadership journey!

CHAPTER 2

Meet Sara: The Coachee

"Whatever chains are holding you back,
don't let them tie you down."

— *One Direction*

Sara is a director-level executive in the head office of a sustainable consumer products company. Sara is looking for new growth opportunities and wants to be promoted to Vice-President. She is reflecting on her recent performance review.

For the third consecutive year, Sara received a great performance review—except she's being told she's not quite strategic enough for the Vice-President level, even though she's been named as a high potential within the organization. Year after year, nothing's changed. She's starting to feel frustrated. She's working hard. She's a good leader. Why is she not being recognized? Sara is seriously considering leaving the organization to pursue opportunities elsewhere.

It's hard for her to hear the same feedback, "Sara, you're not strategic enough" and not know how to help herself. "Not strategic enough": What does that even mean?

This was how her day at work ended today. Clearly, she had some thinking to do, but she didn't even know what to look at. Where to start? What to do? What is she not getting right??

5

On the commute home, she reflects on the events of the past 12 months, trying to see where she wasn't strategic enough. She's just not sure what they mean: she does all the expected budget forecasting and fills out her strategic plan for her team and her projects each year when they're due. And how is she supposed to become more strategic when she doesn't get invited to all those senior leader meetings anyway? Why can't they be specific with what she needs to do to break through this barrier that's keeping her from moving ahead in the organization? Just tell her what to do!

Every year it's the same thing. The same feedback but never the guidance. Sara pours so much of herself into everything she does and yet, when there's an opportunity within the organization, she congratulates someone else for winning a position that she thought could have been hers.

She arrives home, deflated after hearing that she's not strategic enough for the third year in a row, changes into comfortable clothes and starts to prepare dinner. Three consecutive years of this and she's so stuck.

She arrives at work the next morning, having decided that she will talk to her boss Aaron about all this. Maybe there's something the organization can do to help develop her. She feels stagnated and wants some new challenges.

Just as she is sitting down to start her day, Aaron calls her into his office.

"How are you feeling after yesterday's review?" he asks.

After voicing her frustrations, Aaron says, "I don't know if you're aware, but as part of the professional development of our high potential employees, we sometimes offer leadership coaching and, well, we were talking about you and we want to help. What do you think about working with a coach? Someone who can help you to strengthen your strategic capabilities?"

Sara knows she wants this. She knows she needs it and thinks, *YES! Finally, something.*

Aaron continues, "We want to help you develop your talents and see you move up within the organization, and we're willing to invest in making this happen."

Leaning forward, he assures Sara, "I think you have more to offer in terms of the transformational changes our internal culture needs that can help us achieve a competitive advantage in the industry, and frankly for us to become even more of a leader on the big societal and environmental issues we're facing. You are passionate about these bigger change issues, and you lead according to our organizational values and really care for our people. We want more of that in our top leadership! So, if this is something you want, you can work with an external leadership coach who can help you develop your leadership even more, in particular your strategic leadership. I can see you going far within this organization. And we need you leading in this work."

Sara leaves Aaron's office excited for this opportunity, eager to understand where she's missing the mark; where she's *'not strategic enough.'* She also takes comfort in hearing that although she has been passed up for promotions so many times, they still value her and her contributions enough to invest in her. That means something.

Sara is prepared to stretch herself and prove them right. Anything to avoid hearing the same thing at next year's review!

She knows what it took for her to get to this point in her career and be leading a team of ten managers and 350 people. Now it's time to learn what will get her to the next level up and if the organization wants to invest in developing her professionally, she is all in!

This will be Sara's first time working with a coach. She suspects it will be challenging and maybe even a little scary, but mostly she is hopeful that this venture into coaching will be a powerful catalyst to developing more strategic capabilities and enhancing her performance.

CHAPTER 3

Meet Melissa: The Coach

"Strong enough to get it wrong in front of all these people."
— *Louis Tomlinson*

Sara's boss gave Sara a list of coaches to choose from. When she read Melissa Creede's biography, she agreed that she seemed like a great fit. Melissa specializes in coaching those who want to make a bigger impact on important issues, particularly in the spaces of sustainability, climate change, and social justice. Melissa also has a specific expertise in helping leaders become more strategic. And she had developed a couple of others within the organization over recent years and with great success.

In their upcoming sessions together, Melissa will coach Sara on being purposeful and strategic in both her existing and desired roles. Sara can expect to be challenged to widen her perspective, and to move beyond limiting behaviours and beliefs. Ultimately, Melissa will coach Sara to realize the higher potential that is already in her, so she starts shaking up the status quo for the purpose of something better. Sara will grow and create positive change in herself and within her teams, all for the overall benefit of her organization.

Melissa's heartiest desire is to continue developing and catalyzing leaders and changemakers to be more effective in their roles – both inside and outside organizations—to create movements and influence change on important issues and passion projects. She supports them through their journey to discover themselves, the world around them, and their purpose and role in it.

Melissa understands the importance of leadership development. Melissa rose from Project Coordinator to Vice-President in only four years and was an executive by the time she was thirty. She has also coached thousands of leaders and up-and-coming leaders. She knows what it takes to grow. This really appealed to Sara.

Sara will start working with her coach Melissa in two weeks. She has been given five months of coaching and she is determined to make the best of this investment. She knows it is an opportunity not offered to many, and she's convinced this will improve her leadership and catalyze her career.

***

Many organizations want to develop and retain their high performing employees, and such is the case with Sara. Essentially it means that the organization sees her potential to play a more direct role in the transformation of the organization. And this applies at all levels, not just at senior levels.

Sara's aspiration to grow into advanced levels of leadership and make a bigger contribution and impact in her organization, her field, and her passions is about to take on a whole new dimension.

Let's join Melissa and Sara, as Sara works on herself with Melissa's guidance and coaching tools, and gets set to play big and make her corner of the world a better place.

CHAPTER 4

What Does It Mean to Be Strategic in Leadership?

"I believe that one person can make a difference."
— *Greta Thunberg*

Melissa and Sara are meeting for the first of their sessions together.

"Hi Sara," Melissa spoke first. "My name is Melissa, and I'm a leadership coach. I'm excited about working together. Tell me a little bit about why we're here and what I can help you with."

Sara answered, "Well, I just had another performance review and for the third year in a row, I'm listed as a high potential, which is great, but I think I'm kind of stuck there. A high potential who's not realizing her potential, you know? I feel valued by the organization, but I'm very frustrated since I don't know what I need to do to expand all this potential of mine.

"I get really good reviews and I'm given overall feedback, but apparently, I'm not strategic enough. Yet no one has been able to help me understand what that means exactly or what I should be looking at to improve. I think I *am* strategic, so I don't know what to work on. I think that once I get it, I'll be able to move on with new challenges but for now, I'm stagnating."

Melissa smiled at Sara. "Lucky for you, helping leaders be more strategic and connect more with their vision and purpose are my favourite areas to work on. There is a lot we can do and I'm going to help all that potential come out to play.

"First, I want to assure you that this is a confidential arrangement. What goes on here stays between us. This is a open space for us to talk and to work on whatever comes up. I want you to have a place to self-reflect, explore new ideas, share successes, and talk about challenges—without worrying about how that might be perceived by others. That said, let's talk about strategic leadership in general, not necessarily as it applies directly to you."

To speak directly to the question "What does not being strategic enough mean anyway?" Melissa begins to explain what it means to be strategic in leadership, bringing insight into the kinds of things they're going to work on, which are exactly the kinds of abilities and qualities organizations want to see developed in high potential candidates.

When most people in an organization hear the word *strategic*, they think of one or two ways to be strategic: preparing a strategic plan for, instance, or creating a vision statement for their group. They think of these formal and structured tasks of strategic planning. But it's much more than that. 'Being strategic' can actually be pulled apart into several different aspects.

- It's about having a vision for a desired future in whatever areas you lead, and a plan to get there.

- It's about being intentional more than reactive in your day-to-day.
- It's about thinking and reflecting a bit more rather than simply "doing."
- It's about staying in the bigger picture versus getting dragged into the details.
- It's about thinking in the word about here what someone two levels up from you cares about.
- It's about interacting across the business and leading beyond your own initiatives or areas of responsibility.
- It's about showing you can lead above and beyond the operational aspects of the business.

Being strategic could mean many different things, and not all of them have to be considered by all leaders, but generally speaking, a strategic leader has the ability to generate new value, empower direct reports' talent, and provide direction in the way they lead in their own responsibility areas, as well as across the business. It starts with the leader generating value for the organization and their mission, relevant to their role and their level. And it doesn't necessarily mean they have to be strategic in all areas; it just means there are some areas the leader can do so even more, and more broadly, and more intentionally.

And the results can be transformational.

So for Sara, and anyone else for that matter, understanding what strategic leadership means in a given role and within an organization is something important to pay attention to.

It also doesn't mean you need to add to an already hectic schedule; rather it means improving where you spend your time, what you think about, what you pay attention to, and what preoccupies you. You will focus less on purely management and execution issues, and be better at prioritizing bigger issues, delegating work, and eliminating distractions. Being strategic encourages more creative thinking and advancing important projects. In essence, your overall leadership style will be more strategic.

Sara started getting excited hearing this. "I'm ready to start. What do you want to know first?"

"We're going to start with an even bigger picture than just focusing on being more strategic, although I'm certain this will come up given what brought you here." Melissa likes to just jump right in with the big questions:

When you look ahead two to three years, and you think about the kind of leader you want to be: what kind of impact do you want to have? What do you want others to say about you behind your back? What kind of initiatives do you want to be invited to lead and contribute to? Where do you want to add value? What would success look like for you?

Sara closed her eyes for a couple of minutes and reflected on these questions.

From her perspective, success has different dimensions. For Sara to feel successful in her career and in her role as a leader, she wants to know that she's contributing in meaningful ways to the organization, that she's helping other people become better leaders, and that she can stay focused on that instead of being so caught up in the demands of the day-to-day.

Sara expressed that she wants to be known for developing other leaders on her team. And while she's a good people leader, she admitted that far too often she catches herself wanting to make it easier on them. She jumps in to save people, quick to lighten their load, and she has a good sense that this might not always be the best approach for some of her top people. There's so much potential Sara sees in many of her team members, but she's often not great at leveraging their strengths and making the most of their abilities. Sara cares a lot about the people who work with her and for her, and her automatic response is to protect them, even though she knows it's not always the best for them in the long run. Sara was thinking that if she could learn how to balance that by allowing them more rope, it would be good for everyone.

Melissa nodded her head, acknowledging what Sara was saying, "Good. **What else?** "

Sara paused then admitted, with some hesitation, "I wish I knew how to be more visionary. I know that's probably a weird thing to say out loud, but I do think that this is a weakness that holds me back. I want to come up with something that pushes the organization's potential—make us think bigger about what we *could* be. I want to be able to better articulate my wildest imaginations for what could be created at some point in the future in a way that others are excited about and committed to. And then, of course, to be recognized for it. But it's hard to do. And I never seem to have the time to focus on this, probably because it's not even a well-defined thing yet.

"And I wish I had more time. How am I supposed to find the time to create something new? Most days I'm just running from meeting to meeting with barely a minute to grab a glass of water or even take a breath.

"And I always want to be available for my people—I have ten managers and between them about 350 people, so they're a priority for me. But some days it just feels like I'm pulled in too many directions. I get messages or calls to help my employees solve problems or deal with an issue that comes up unexpectedly, or sometimes I get requests from my senior team or the board, and my entire day is derailed. It's all important stuff; it just doesn't leave much room for visionary work.

"Also, I wish I was better at articulating my proposals and thoughts, both to my higher ups and my direct reports. I don't think I'm a bad communicator in general, but many times, when I make a suggestion, it doesn't seem to really land. Often, I think that no one cares about what I care about. But to me it's so obvious. Maybe I need to be a better communicator."

Smiling, Melissa said, "It sounds even more like you want to be a better influencer—get others to adopt your suggestions with enthusiasm. Let's keep going. **What else do you want to be known for?**"

Sara thought some more. "I think I am already appreciated for being a person of integrity. I do what I say I'm going to do. I think I have really good interpersonal skills—sometimes I think maybe almost too much because I really don't want to burden people when I can see they're overloaded or have too much on their plates. My empathy is pretty high. I'm known as a caring leader—and I definitely don't want to lose that. I love that I have this reputation, but I want more. I would love to be known for spearheading a new initiative, something exciting and impactful, something that makes a big difference and that outlasts me."

Melissa said, "These are amazing qualities. I can understand why the organization wants you as one of their top leaders. **What else do you want people to be saying about you?**"

"This goes back again to the word integrity," Sara added. "I'd love people to be saying that I am fair and honest and reliable and that they can trust me. That I'm loyal. A good mentor, someone who will push others to see and utilize their potential. Someone who is approachable, that they respect but are not afraid of."

Melissa asked, **"What do you want your colleagues to be thinking about you, to be looking for from you when they invite you into a meeting?"**

"I believe I am a creative and critical thinker and that bodes well in many of the meetings I've been invited to," Sara told her. "I'm good at looking at the facts and figuring out some solutions, and I'm not afraid to contribute new ideas to the conversation that are often pivotal in leading us away from or towards decisions that we're there to make. I think I'm valued for such types of contributions. I like that, so I'd want them to keep thinking and saying those things. Honestly? I'd also love it if I was known for something no one else has, you know, like 'go to Sara for that. It's her superpower'."

Melissa wanted Sara to see that when she gives this question a little space and time to think about—for any circumstance or issue—how much more exciting and clear the vision becomes.

Only 10 minutes into the session and Sara easily started to articulate much of **'what success would look like?'** about her leadership. This is a giant step into awareness that will precede the changes she so much wants to make. She's starting to identify the things that look like success to her, which then becomes her own personal vision of her leadership. With a personal vision of leadership, it's easier to identify what needs to be developed and grow from there.

Going back to the concept of her superpower, Melissa asked Sara, **"What do you think people would say now about "that's Sara's superpower?"**

"Hmmm…" Sara thought, "They would probably say they come to me when they need to work through something. I'm a good problem solver. That's probably my superpower. People come to me for that, they rely on me for that.

"Oh, and I'm also really good at communicating expectations, goals, and objectives to my team. I spend a lot of time fleshing it all out so we're all on the same page. The team walks away from our planning meetings with no doubts as to what we are setting out to do and how to go about it and when to deliver. I'm not sure if that's my superpower, but I'm good at it."

Melissa responded, "Every leader, regardless of where they fall on the spectrum of strategic leadership, has some really great strengths to play with. You have your own unique set of skills that are recognized and valued by the organization. And, sometimes these very qualities may also be distracting you from being seen as strategic. These skills may involve a lot of 'reacting' to situations and problems, 'fixing' problems, 'saving' people and proposing solutions. These are definitely not bad qualities, in fact they're valued and even celebrated, but in a general sense, these can sometimes be in tension with being strategic. Why? Because these are not as intentional, not as forward-thinking, not as big picture and not as long-term, and therefore, not as strategic.

"And again, clarity around expectations is likely very much appreciated and no one wants you to stop doing that, but you want to make sure you're not being drawn into the tactical unintentionally, rather than staying at the strategic level. Perhaps a manager or another direct report could be doing some of the more detailed planning. Essentially, it's about keeping your natural strengths and value-added highly present—we don't want to throw those away—but also taking a more strategic approach.

"When I ask, '**What's your brand or reputation?**', if you say 'I have a good reputation' and leave it at that, you may not be taking full advantage of what you could be exploring with this question. It's not really about whether or not your reputation is good or bad. If you are a leader on a high-potential list, or you are recognized for your contributions to your organization or your team, or if you get good performance reviews, you likely have a good, if not great, reputation. The question to really consider is 'does your reputation (or brand) match what you want to be known for, and what you want to lead and what you want to do next?' Oftentimes it doesn't."

The next position up for Sara is Vice-President and so for her, does that position need a problem solver/helper/fixer/planner alone or does it need a visionary, a forward thinker, a strategic thinker on top of all those already established attributes? Does her current reputation set her up to be considered for the role of VP? I'd say no.

Speaking to Sara, Melissa said, "Let's put into practice some real ways to adjust how you show up day-to-day. And let's keep exploring **'What does success look like two to three years from now as a leader?' 'What kind of impact do you want to have as a leader?'"**

Before meeting Melissa, Sara had only surfaced these questions, never really digging into answers, but now, being asked by her coach to actually talk it out, was already somehow helping crystallize what she wants.

For where Sara is right now in her career, she has two answers. One, as mentioned, on the people-side of things, she wants to be known as someone who makes lasting changes in developing people. It's important for Sara to be known for helping others thrive in their own versions of leadership. To be known for easily and readily helping people operate at their highest potential. To be known for getting people excited about their growth and development. And to be a leader that people are excited about working with. More than anything, it would mean the world to her to know that overall, she has a positive influence on people by helping them to develop their own leadership abilities.

The other response, more on the passion and purpose side of things, Sara wants to make real and lasting change in something meaningful in the world—something that affects society at large. Her organization and products are a big part of that. They're formulating sustainable, eco-friendly products that have the potential for real transformative change and they're contributing to making households healthier, resulting in a healthier planet. That's what attracted Sara to this organization in the first place, and so, the more successful they are, the better the world becomes. And she wants to make sure that her own leadership has a direct impact on all of that — to keep pushing the organization to up their game, to be innovative in materials, ideas, designs, approaches, and partnerships. She wants them to be leaders in making and holding up to sustainability commitments, in their greenhouse gas reductions, diversity and inclusion efforts, human rights stances—internally and with our partners and suppliers. And deep down, she also wants them to be bolder—to really lead and transform their industry even though she's not always sure how.

"So, you see," Sara finished with, "That's the stuff that really drives my passions and purpose."

"This is so great!" Melissa got excited right along with her. "I can hear the excitement in your voice, and you seem energized just by talking about it. I also hear your personal values and purpose coming out—that's huge. We've got to get you there so you can contribute even more greatly to the cause."

The good news is that Sara mentioned some pieces of being strategic: having a vision for a desired future is forward-looking, it's aligned to her organization's mission and purpose, and it is intentional. She just needs a little help staying strategic and not being distracted by her to-do list.

Just then Sara spoke up, admitting, "My excitement lasts a minute and then, I have to be honest, most days I just end up trying to get through meetings, or my emails, or my to-do list."

This is an all-too familiar trap every leader falls into at least some of the time, if not daily. Leading teams, answering to higher ups, attending meetings, being there for their people, and frankly just getting through their in-box make for very full days and keeps people super busy. What typically happens? Most people go right into action mode. Do, do, do. React, React, React. Answer. Answer. Answer. Emails. Phone calls. Meetings. Meetings. Deadlines. Responding to other people who need answers and solutions and action now. In an hour from now. Attending to all of the day-to-day stuff that needs doing, which is great but it's coming at a cost.

Melissa said with a smile, "This is all very familiar. Don't worry. You'll get there. Like a good strategic coach, I'd like to start with the big picture, the ideal end-state. The best version or vision of the future you can imagine. In fact, we've already started. You've given some great answers to my questions, so let's turn these into some **Leadership Goals**. And then pair these with some really practical, tangible, doable actions. So, we'll create a **Leadership Action Plan** to guide you in your leadership journey."

The Leadership Action Plan

<u>Step 1</u> is to define **what success would look like for your leadership** two to three years from now. Really paint the picture. Be bold. Think big. **What are your aspirations? What does your leadership look like in two to three years? What do you want your reputation to be? What impact do you want to be having? What kind of work do you want to be doing? What do you want others to be thinking about you and saying about you? What do you want them to consider you for or invite you to? What do you want your direct reports to be saying about you?** Think of the best version of the future you can imagine. This is your **Leadership Vision**.

The **Leadership Vision** is a combination of the type of leader you want to *be* as well as what you want to *do* as a leader.

Next, do a self-assessment, a check-in, on where you are with this vision. If two to three years from now, you were seen as all of the things you just described, if that's your 10/10 vision, what would you score yourself now out of 10 compared to that list?

<u>Step 2a</u> is to identify two to three **Leadership Goals** – those areas you want to focus on that will get you closer to your **Leadership Vision**. As I alluded to, these are not necessarily your weaknesses: these are areas of focus that will have the *most* impact in helping you become the leader you want to become and have the impact you want to have.

These aren't performance goals, or short-term goals for delivery, but rather goals that help you become the leader you want to be. They're more about your growth as a leader rather than a specific thing you are going to accomplish. And we want to make sure that the leadership goal isn't actually an action disguised as a goal. For instance, 'delegating more' is an action, not a growth goal.

<u>Step 2b</u> is to further define the **Leadership Goal** in a way that would help get closer to the **Leadership Vision**. Let's say you want to be a more strategic leader.

It's important to really tease out your vision of what being a more strategic leader looks like. Most leadership goals are hard to measure, but the truth is, many very worthwhile things are hard to measure. Thus, we answer **"What would success look like or what's the after-picture look like"** for Goal 1. **What will you notice if you are more strategic?** How will you act? How will others interact with you? What will you do differently in terms of your day-to-day efforts? How will you show up in meetings and interactions? What do you want to see happening? From my point of view, we're looking for progress.

You're never going to "achieve" being strategic – it's not something you reach and then you're done – but you will become more strategic over time. It's also really important to notice the little changes in your behaviours and actions and impact. This helps you do that.

Step 2c is to rate yourself out of 10 for each goal. In this case, for Goal 1 – how strategic you are now, compared to the list of what you described success to look like for that particular goal. Just like we did for the overall Leadership Vision, but for each of the three goals. This is a simple way to track progress over time. Even though it's just a simple and subjective self-rating, it does give you a sense of where you are now compared to where you want to be. It also creates a tension between where you are now and where you want to be which helps propel you into action.

Step 3 is to connect with *why* this goal is important to your leadership success. This, combined with "what would success look like" (step 2b) for the goal helps motivate you to *want* to focus some energy on this.

Step 4 is the last step for this Goal 1, the Action step: **What specific actions could you take today and tomorrow and next week that will help you get closer to the 10/10 vision for this "what would success look like" criteria?**

That's the part that brings this from ideas to tangible actions. There are specific actions and specific strategies that people can take to be more strategic and not just for big initiatives, or for yearly strategic plans, but also on a day-to-day basis, in every meeting, in every conversation, every day. This also helps turn something big picture and nebulous and a bit hard to measure into something you can track easily on a day-to-day basis. It allows you to consider: "Did I actually do something specific today that helps me get closer to my leadership vision?"

Then repeat steps two through four for one or two other goals until you have no more than three leadership goals in total that help you grow and evolve into the **Leadership Vision** you've set out for yourself. We'll be focusing on the goal of being more strategic throughout this book but creating one or two additional goals is recommended. Other leadership goals might relate to: being more influential, developing talent or a high performing team, or creating a culture in which everyone can thrive, to name a few. And these will all overlap with the goal of being strategic as well. They are interconnected. None of them is achieved in isolation. In fact, most of these other examples of leadership goals will be present in our "strategic" goal as well.

If you do a good job with these leadership goals, they should actually be quite relevant for a year or two (even though you might modify any of the steps a little as you go). Usually, the actions and strategies evolve the most over time as you adopt better leadership habits.

***

Now, let's see what this looks like using Sara's first Leadership Goal which was defined as, "I am a strategic and intentional leader."

Melissa asked Sara, "Let's further define your Goal 1: I am a strategic and intentional leader. Let's also look at how being more strategic can actually save you time, make you less busy with the daily urgent things that drain you so you can be more focused on strategic future-oriented things that excite you.

"What would you say success would look like if you were even more of a strategic leader?

Sara responded with, "Spending time thinking and reflecting more than just doing and executing."

Melissa loved this answer and urged Sara on to come up with more of what she envisions for herself. Sara struggled to come up with anything, so Melissa prodded her, asking, "What about being intentional more than reactive?"

Sara jumped at that point. "I want to do more than just fight fires and respond to others' requests. I want to figure out how to be more future-focused and not always caught up in the present. I also always want to keep the big picture in mind."

Melissa was thrilled for Sara because already, in just this first session she could foresee that Sara was going to advance quickly in their work together.

The metaview, the whole forest, not just the trees, taking a "birds-eye" view or even the 10,000 foot level... These are all common metaphors that imply the same thing. It also means not only being focused on the details and the tactical. This might mean looking at the project you're leading from the perspective of the next two years, rather than the part that has to be done this week. Or seeing the two or three bigger themes that are emerging in a conversation rather than just the details being described. It might mean seeing how the areas you're leading interact with another area of the business that might not at first be obvious.

Sara also asked, "I would imagine being strategic includes participating in the formal annual planning process or being involved in creating an overall strategy for the organization, right? And maybe linking those to organizational or team goals?"

"Yes, also very important," Melissa continued. "We can be strategic in the day-to-day, which is what we've been talking about so far, and we can also follow formal processes and requirements for strategic planning typically once or twice year. Sometimes I look at this one as having a vision and purpose, and then a plan to get there. And yes, this can be at the organizational level, at the senior leadership team level, but it could also be for your department and/or your team. And then it's important to cascade individual and team goals up with project goals and department goals and ensuring they're also aligned with broader organizational goals, values, mission, or other stated aims. It's a way to make sure the strategic pieces are integrated throughout the organization."

That's when Sara remembered something her boss sometimes reminded her to do. He often told her to find more time to interact with her peers. This was something Sara struggled with—as many leaders do—yet, she knows has something to do with being strategic, and Melissa agrees.

Peer interaction is an excellent habit for many reasons (influence, collaboration, etc.) but the part that relates to being strategic especially is that it's important to see beyond your role and across the organization. It helps to see interconnectedness rather than silos. Meeting with peers is one action that helps a leader do that. And being intentional in those meetings is important too. **What are the bigger initiatives they are trying to move forward over the course of six months or a year? What is the link between those initiatives and the broader organizational goals? What are the interconnections and overlaps with your area? What are your peers' priorities? What keeps them up at night? What are their challenges? What themes are you noticing?**

In future sessions, we will look at how to focus on the strategic things more than other urgent priorities. We'll explore recognizing and anticipating trends inside and outside the company and the sector. And how to think more like the senior leaders in the organization.

A good strategic leader doesn't have to be all these things we've been talking about. It depends on their level, their responsibilities, who else is on their leadership team, and many other considerations. Most leaders I meet want to improve the way they lead but they keep getting derailed and they can't see why. By bringing awareness into what they think about, what they talk about, and where they spend their time, they can develop strategic ways to avoid the common derailers, realign themselves and start to realize their full potential.

We're going to explore all of this in this book, and you can choose a few to focus your attention on that are most important to you to really elevate your leadership. You'll start to see where your time and energy goes so you can be more deliberate—more intentional—to have even greater impact. You'll become more strategic about how you think. You'll start putting more attention to what you want to create instead of what you want to fix. All of this will keep you from getting caught up in the day-to-day minutiae of overseeing and executing.

We'll also continue to come up with actions and strategies to do on a day-to-day basis to shift your leadership to be more strategic.

Melissa said, "There are more ways to define success and there are more actions that we'll look at later for this too, but this is probably a great place to end today."

Sara nodded. "I'm really starting to see already how I had such a narrow view of being strategic, and really hadn't thought through all these elements. I wish I had figured this out before. But it's exciting and I know the work I do with you will make a difference. I'm starting to understand what the feedback I've been getting means. That's the one hand. On the other hand, making time for this is a concern. How am I going to fit this in? I barely have a minute to myself as it is—my days are already full. I want to get to a point where I'm less involved in the day-to-day but accomplishing more, if that makes any sense, and it's weird, you know, because I can imagine it. But how?"

Getting less involved in the day-to-day activities is a common desire among busy people. Many people get promoted because they're great implementers. They get stuff done. They're there to help the organization and their peers through the problems and the fires. Does any of this sound familiar: letting deadlines, urgent requests, emails, and messages drive your day rather than an intentional idea of what is important to move forward in a day? Letting your inbox and to-do list drive your decisions and actions rather than being in conscious choice. Waiting for time to "free up" for you so you can work on your more important things? Not knowing what your longer-term priorities are, and therefore not prioritizing them? Don't feel bad, these are very common derailers for many, many people, at all levels within organizations.

But here's the thing: When you develop new skills around this, you end up with more time, even though it doesn't seem like it at this point. And you end up with more energy. It's exhausting to run from urgent task to urgent task all day, responding and reacting to every request or problem. It's not as effective either. Trust me when I tell you that you will actually have more time to focus on the areas that matter more in the longer term. And you won't feel as frantic, as reactive. We will identify and put into practice the strategies that will help you with this. We will identify common derailers that get in the way. You'll adopt new patterns of thinking, behaving, and doing. You gain a new vision for success to be the leader you want to be—the one you defined today, and some tools, habits and strategies to get there. That future you, that future leader is right at your fingertips.

Melissa said: "Sara, next time we will explore these leadership goals even more, but I want you to leave with at least a couple of actions to try between now and then. I know we've gone through a lot today. But the work we're doing in these initial sessions is going to really pave the way for success.

"First, take a bit of time to reflect on your **Leadership Vision (Step 1): What kind of leader do I want to be? What kind of impact would I be making? What's exciting? How do I want to be?** Really imagine yourself as that leader. Ideally, you'd write this out in a journal, or do something creative with it, have a conversation with a colleague or loved one, if you're more visual, tap into that–anything to help you really connect with this. One of my favourite exercises is to write a letter to yourself today from yourself five years in the future–write it in long-hand cursive, if possible, not typed on the computer. Tell yourself what kind of leader you are, what kind of impact you're having–all the questions we've talked about. You'll have my notes from today, so you have a great starting point. We've already started defining your **Leadership Vision**; just really imagine it and connect with it.

"Second, start to fill out the **Leadership Action Plan** I'm sending you. It has all the steps we've discussed. We've started to tease out Goal 1: I am a strategic and intentional leader. Do the same for two other goals following Steps two, three, and four. Don't worry about getting everything perfect. Just start to fill this in. Use your **Leadership Vision** for guidance for these three goals. Once you do the **Leadership Vision** exercise in more depth, these other two goals will emerge quite obviously. Steps two and three will be more evident.

"Today's session was longer–a double session in fact–and this homework is a bit longer and more intense than most of our other sessions will be. As I said already, spending a bit more time on this at the front-end will really propel you to the leader you want to be more quickly.

"Lastly, I want to leave you with a very simple action you could start practicing between now and next time. Try to use this at least a few times a day and it only takes 10 seconds. Ask the question (out loud to others in conversations or even silently to yourself): ***what would success look like?*** You could ask this question in so many circumstances: in a meeting when everyone is going in different directions; with a direct report who is looking to you for guidance; with your boss if you want to make sure you're both seeing the same direction and end-state;

if you're working on a project plan and want to make sure all the milestones along the way lead to the right outcome; with a client if you want to make sure what you're providing to them is what they actually need. It's actually my favourite question and it has so many uses. Just start using it. A lot. Especially if you feel yourself drawn into a problem that needs fixing, this is a great way to step into the big picture, the future, the meta-view. It's a great question to help you be more strategic in the moment. And it will help you, and others, envision what you want to move towards, the desired future rather than just what you're fixing. Reflecting on this question will start a subtle shift towards what you want to create rather than just what you want to fix, and it will start you on the path of making a big difference."

Before leaving Sara said, "This homework you're leaving me with reminds me of when I was in grade six and our art teacher made us create a vision board using cut outs from magazines. I'm excited to play with it."

CHAPTER 5

Intentional Thinking Versus Being Reactive

"I'm so sick of running as fast as I can."

— *Taylor Swift*

Most leaders fall into patterns of being "on" all the time, always running from meeting to meeting, answering emails and messages, and doing whatever is expected of them typically in an urgent way. Instead, let's look at what can improve when you take a step back to bring more intentionality to the "doing." Sara has mentioned that she is a big problem solver. She has also said that she is so busy that it's hard to find time to think or reflect on some of the bigger areas on which she wants to make an impact.

Spending time deliberately thinking provides the space for you to pause before acting. It helps you imagine and define the desired future, a vision, that you want to move to and come up with strategies to move in that direction. Being intentional with your time allows you to stay focused on the most important issues that **you** want and need to focus on over the longer term. It allows you to make more informed decisions. And, most importantly, it helps you stay in the big picture, and stay connected with the desired future, the end-state you're moving towards rather than just reacting to everything that crosses your path.

Scheduling time for intentional (and typically strategic) thinking, reflecting, and planning might feel like another thing you're adding to your to-do list, but it's not really in the same category. It doesn't have to be a lot of time. As with anything new, once you start, the habit gets formed and once you see the results of this, it becomes something you're not willing to give up. And you'll be less frenzied, more focused, get better results, and typically feel more in balance and less frantically busy. Instead of thinking of it as added time, think of it as time moved forward – it replaces frantic time later.

In today's session Melissa and Sara briefly catch up on the few weeks that have passed.

"Hi Sara," Melissa starts, "It's good to see you again. How have you been?"

"Mostly good," Sara settles into the conversation, "Actually, I had a hectic few weeks dealing with a delivery issue so there was that, but I tried to do what we talked about last time."

"Fantastic! I'm looking forward to hearing more." Melissa then asked, "**What successes have you had since last time?**"

Sara thought for a minute, "Well, for one, I wrote a letter to myself as you had asked me to do."

What impact did writing a letter to herself have on Sara about what kind of leader she wants to be? Let's explore this a bit.

Having to intentionally dig into the question of what kind of leader Sara wanted to be was enlightening. She told Melissa it caused her to think a little more deeply about the impact she wants to have and to draw out in finer detail what success would be for her as a leader. It was the first time she deliberately took time to think about that, and Sara admitted that for the first time ever she really connected to this aspirational version of herself and her leadership. It wasn't that much new came out of it during the journaling process; rather, it was that she gained so much clarity around her aspirations and what that might look like and how she might get there. It was a much more visceral experience with a much stronger pull. It's almost like she could taste it. Taking the time to think and write caused a stir in her that now, she couldn't wait to make that happen.

"Oh, wow," Melissa jumped in, "that's exactly what's supposed to happen! And to assure you, we don't typically expect big or new A-HAs to come out of the blue for people; it's more like the extra noise falls away and we're left with the truest version of ourselves and our desires."

"Exactly!" Sara added, "The stuff that came up for me was a combination of desires: that I want to enable others to help them be at their best, that I want to be seen as strategic and visionary and intentional, that I want to make a difference in the sustainability sector. These aren't necessarily new ideas, but

I don't think I had ever been able to name them so clearly, and I didn't have such motivation or drive to really step into that leadership without being distracted by the day-to-day. I know for sure I will want to keep building on this experience, keep fanning the flames of this desire.

"But I also remember, Melissa, that you also asked me to set aside time for planning. I didn't do very well with that."

"Okay," Melissa answered her. "We're looking for progress and momentum, not perfection! So, what did you get to?"

Sara said, "I was able to steal away 15 minutes to prepare for an important meeting, but that's all the time I had."

"Well, that's a success!" Melissa reassured her. "It's 15 minutes of preparation that you probably wouldn't have done before our conversation, which makes it something to celebrate. What was the impact of those few minutes of prep time?"

Sara thought about it and realized that she felt less stressed going into the meeting and even more in charge of herself while she was there. She contributed to the conversation right from the start and attributed her confidence to the mental prep work she had done prior to going into the meeting.

From a strategic point of view, Sara had envisioned being in the meeting as if it were already taking place. She had reflected on the purpose of the meeting, what they were all there for, and where she could add the most value. She thought about each of the decision makers, where they would be seated, what would be emphasized at the meeting, essentially imagining the unfolding dynamic of it. In the past, Sara would have prepared the details or content she wanted to share, or updates about her projects, but this time she also looked at the bigger picture. She reflected on: **What's the purpose of the meeting? What would success look like by the end of the meeting?** She also thought about the projects she's responsible for and what the senior people around the table would really need to know.

She also took 20 or 30 seconds to deliberately think about and intentionally choose: **How do I want to show up in this meeting? What role do I want to play? What value do I want to contribute? Who do I want to <u>be</u> versus what do I want to <u>do</u>?** She decided she wanted to be seen as "strategic thinker and contributor" rather than "expert" and noticed that for the first time, her energy shifted and dialogue changed to fit the vision she intentionally chose. And that was just from a 30-second intention on how she wanted to show up, to *be*, in the meeting.

Also, since she didn't rush from her previous meeting and instead, took a bit of time between what she was doing before the meeting to ground herself, she was less frazzled going into it. Her head was clearer, she felt fully present and engaged, and she was able to add to the meeting with confidence. Sara felt that strategically that this was a big win for her, and this set her on a path to seek out what more could happen for her if she were to take the time to get grounded and strategically prepare herself more before going into all meetings.

Imagine if everyone in business reflected on these kinds of questions before meetings how much more effective all meetings would be. Instead of spending the first 15 minutes trying to figure out what the meeting is about, what the outcome should be, and why they're even there, everyone would be prepared and ready to have meaningful conversations and make things happen.

Now that Sara had the experience of a much better meeting because of the thinking she did before going into it, she started to think about other types of things in her world that would benefit from some additional thinking and reflection time.

Going forward, she will definitely prepare more strategically for meetings as she now knows that this is the way to go. This quick but intentional prep work made her a more effective, higher-level contributor. She felt more in charge of herself and more strategic and was also *seen* as being more strategic. She felt so good to know that she added more value. To take the learning even a step further, Sara could see how much more productive and meaningful meetings could be if people took the time to think ahead to the purpose, meaning, and intention of meetings, and what value they can contribute before entering into them. This helps everyone.

Melissa congratulated Sara on such a big win for such a small action. She added, "You've seen how just reflecting on a few strategic questions before a meeting can make all the difference. And you've seen it doesn't even have to take a long time. I'm going to remind you often: being intentional is a big part of being strategic. Knowing this now as you do, **what other**

areas do you think could benefit from some thinking time, planning time, strategic time?

Without a moment's pause, Sara quickly answered, "Career development of my staff. I need to do some thinking about the goals we've discussed, any feedback I need to give them, recognition that I might not have passed on yet, what our resource plan for the next six months looks like, their own career aspirations. Things like that. In fact, for my second leadership goal in the Leadership Action Plan, I've started to define a goal I called: I develop talent and enable high performance. I started filling in that goal and I am really motivated by it because you know that's really exciting to me."

"That's excellent. We'll work on that goal together too. But let's keep going with the strategic goal. **What else will benefit from strategic thinking?** " Melissa asked.

"There's this really big initiative that I'm leading for the organization that's just getting started." Sara continued, "I really need to sit down and think through the bigger picture of this, what are all the pieces, what I need to accomplish, who the other stakeholders are. A whole bunch of things really. And there's also budget planning for next year that's calling my attention. Oh, and I also have to write a strategic plan with my counterpart for the areas we oversee. And there is a large, complex project that I'm leading that I just need to sit and think through where we're heading, what risks and barriers we might face, how we're going to get it done in the timeframe asked–the whole thing really."

"Okay," Melissa said, "All good examples of activities that require a bit of extra thinking and planning before they become urgent."

All these things will require different amounts of time. You might have to tackle some on a weekly basis or put in a significant amount of time for two weeks but then not again for a couple months, or sometimes just a few minutes before an important discussion. You'll have a better handle on this once you spend some time with these strategic thinking activities, but the key is to just start. I know that sounds silly or obvious, but most of us wait and hope we're going to magically free up some time, or have a lull in the day, but that never really happens, does it?

For now, let's start with meetings, since meetings are typically a big part of almost every leader's day. It will depend on the type of meeting but for most, even just 10-15 minutes of reflection or preparation can make a difference. And remember, it's also *what* you prepare: are you preparing just to answer questions about content or details, or are you thinking strategically as we mentioned:

- **What's the purpose of the meeting?**
- **What would success look like by the end of the meeting?**
- **Who are the decision makers and who are the influencers in the meeting?**

- **What are their perspectives and wants and pain points?**
- **What value can you add and if you were invited, what value are you expected to add? What's the connection to what's being discussed in the meeting and what you're in charge of?**
- **What are the few questions you want to ask others or the main messages you want to get across?**

This might sound like a lot, but most of the time, it will likely only take you a couple minutes to think through these questions.

There are a few ways to fit this thinking time in. For really important meetings, book the 15-20 minutes before the meeting to prepare—or if you need time to absorb what you're reflecting on, book 15-20 minutes the previous day or earlier in the week. You may have to move some meetings, but ideally when the meeting is booked, go ahead and book the additional thinking time in your calendar right away. If it's a recurring meeting, add that to the calendar to recur with the meeting. Even if you really don't have much time, just reflecting on this for a few minutes makes a big difference.

It's a good practice to deliberately end all one-hour meetings at the forty-five-minute mark so everyone can get ready for their next meeting, take a break, or whatever. That means starting to wrap up that meeting no later than the 35-minute mark, not at the last minute. If you're running the meeting, make that your goal. If you're not running the meeting but 45-minutes was agreed upon ahead of time, at 35-minutes you can say something like, "We only have 10 minutes left before we wrap up. Can we make sure we're all clear on our commitments leaving here?"

Ideally, you also want to book time in your calendar throughout your week for thinking and preparing for different things, not just meetings. Maybe you want to block out two hours Friday afternoon for some longer-term planning, or you want to spend thirty minutes on Monday morning to do some weekly planning, or you might want to use a block of time to think through a particular project.

Book these meetings now and also recurring far into the future so the time is already reserved before your calendar gets filled up. It will take a bit of intention for you to fully integrate this into your calendar and your habits, and also to figure out what tends to work best for you. As you start to make this a practice, you'll instinctively start knowing what you need in terms of time to prepare, what works best in your calendar, and managing your own natural energy ebbs and flows.

The reality is that most leaders spend very little or no time just thinking and reflecting. Workplaces are set up for busy, busy, busy and doing, doing, doing. "Doing" is a frenetic energy. It feels productive; it feels like you're getting stuff done. Thinking allows you to be more intentional.

Without thinking, you tend to be more reactive; you tend to just have a long to-do list of tasks without really knowing how they all fit together.

Warren Buffet, one the richest self-made men in the world, has said he spent about 80 percent of his time thinking and reading. Most of us can't even imagine that kind of time spent on something that's not in execution mode.

Deliberate, intentional, strategic thinking time is essential to your work. It's productive time that you slot for reflection, creation, innovation, planning, and whatever you feel needs your attention. This is not something that you want spilling into your family and leisure time. It's not something that you add on that will extend your workday or steal time away from your down time. Ideally, you don't want to relegate this on your commute into work or at night before going to bed. Of course, you *can* spend time on your commute thinking, but this is also a valid and necessary part of your workday. Treat it as such.

Here are a few other tips I've learned over the years:

It's best to use the first few weeks for experimentation. Play with the length of time and the times of day to see when you do your best thinking, but also to see what sticks. Maybe you think a two-hour chunk of time is what you need, but you discover that a few 15- and 30-minute slots work better. Maybe you have good intentions for Monday mornings, but it never works out to be a good time. Give yourself the flexibility to change it.

Book twice more time as you think you need. If you think you need three hours a week, book six hours. It's inevitable that some of it will get taken over by other last minute and urgent needs. But if you book six hours and still end up spending two or three hours, you're still doing more than you're doing now.

And actually put this on your calendar. You must reserve it. You will never "find" time to do this. You just won't. Book it out as far as you can. It's a lot easier to book time in your calendar three or four weeks from now or two months from now than this week. Book that time now.

Give it a name that reflects its importance. If other people have access to your calendar, name it something other than "me time" or "thinking time" or just a blank block of time. Name it something that feels a bit more tangible or important. Otherwise, others will see this as "free time." If it's not named something important, they'll decide for you that their issue is more important. Proactively tell others that these blocks of time are off-limits and why–normalize that this time is important. If it's too far out in the calendar for you to know what you're working on, you could call it "strategic planning" or "project planning" or something like that. It doesn't matter if when the time comes, you decide there is something else strategic to spend that time on. What matters most is that you book it and protect it.

Create a Strategic To-Do List. Make a list of things you want to use that time for: things that require some extra reflection, some focused planning time. Many of us might get as far as blocking off the time but then, when the time comes, we're not even sure what we're supposed to be spending that time on. Either our mind goes blank or it's all over the place. So make a list of six or seven things that require this kind of attention and thinking, and as more ideas come to you, keep adding to the list. The ideas will start in your mind, but create the list and write them down, adding more as they come up. You want to build a list of possible strategic things to actually spend your time on. The key word is *strategic*. It's not to catch up on your emails (although you may need to book additional time for that too) and it's not to pump out something urgent that someone just dropped on your desk (although that will happen sometimes too). But once you do sit down to think and plan and reflect, it will be a lot easier if you have at your fingertips some of the important things you need to pay attention to. And remember, this is NOT your regular to-do list. This is your **Strategic To-Do List.**

Each week when you're planning out the week, take the time you've already pre-booked in your calendar, and assign a specific activity that you want to focus on this week. It should be strategic, longer term, important, but still specific. In the same way others will see "free time" or unassigned time as something unimportant, your own brain will too. If it doesn't have something assigned to it in your mind (as well as ideally in your actual calendar), it's much more likely that you will replace it with something urgent that has to get done. Instead, you want to protect that time for something strategic and meaningful. For instance, if you have a three-hour block of time recurring every Friday morning for Strategic Planning, at the beginning of the week, you might assign the time this week to "resource planning for Q3" or "project ABC roadmap." Or you could assign the one hour you booked next Monday morning to come up with a draft plan for communicating a new initiative. Or during that 15-minute time slot you booked this Wednesday, you could plan to write up a few talking points or feedback or recognition that you want to communicate to each of your direct reports. On your Friday afternoon time slot this coming week, decide that you'll reflect on what resources might be needed over the next six months. And remember, it's perfectly okay to change your mind when that time comes if you decide to use that time for something else strategic or big picture. The purpose of assigning of a specific strategic activity is to protect the time in your mind, as well as give you a head start if you aren't sure what to use the time for. If your energy and attention need to go elsewhere, it's okay, especially if the new things to focus on are also strategic and longer term—as long as its intentional! (Some of the examples mentioned here might seem tangible or be actual deliverables, but they're still strategic in nature in that they're thinking through a bigger picture or forward-looking perspective. And ideally, you're doing them long before they're urgent).

I know your schedule might be crazy right now, and this might feel impossible at the moment. But essentially, time management is simply where you choose to spend your time. It's a simple concept but not always easy to implement.

Be intentional about what you're choosing.

I know this is easier to say than to do most of the time. I often hear clients say, "I just need to free up some time," but the reality is that this will never happen. Your to-do list is not going to get shorter. You will not finish everything by the end of today or tomorrow—or anytime really. You just need to choose to do this instead of something else, even if that something else is urgent. And part of that means blocking out some time in your calendar so it's not quite as hard. It's not the only way, but it will help. Most of us live by our calendars, so let your calendar help you.

Nodding in agreement because what Melissa explained made sense and sometimes, shaking her head with overwhelm, Sara took notes, absorbing it all. "These are all good ideas but just a point of clarification: Do these all have to be things that are due a long time from now, or can they also be things that need my attention now?"

Melissa answered, "That's a great question. Some things are both strategic and urgent. For example, next year's strategic plan that is due tomorrow… that probably feels pretty urgent. So do those performance reviews that have to be submitted to a system by this upcoming Monday. Again, this becomes urgent. The ideal scenario is to tackle these things before they become urgent. They might be things that you eventually have to do as a deliverable but getting to them before they become time sensitive is the more strategic approach. And often you can be more strategic in your day-to-day activities; it's kind of like what you told me at the start of this session about how your 15 minutes of thinking time helped you with your mindset in the meeting."

Sara felt energized about the prospect of spending time on some of these things. She wasn't sure, though, how it would go practically, especially with regard to her team.

"You know, Melissa," Sara pondered aloud, "this thought popped into my head. I should also be thinking about my team, right? Like, how are my people doing according to their career goals? Feedback and recognition happen pretty haphazardly around here, and I know I can do better with that, too."

"For sure you can," Melissa agreed. "And with this time scheduled in your calendar you're giving yourself the time to think about your people, which is something I know is important to you. You can slate it for whatever comes up. If you have performance reviews once a year, quarterly you can reflect on where they are and make notes of this. And you can communicate all this to them too. Feedback and recognition should happen frequently—even weekly. Everyone can benefit from additional feedback and recognition."

There's no end to how blocking off time to think can help leaders strategically move themselves and their people forward. Developing this as a strategy moves everyone closer toward creating impact—even if it's by speaking up at one more meeting as a result of this blocked-off time.

"Well, Melissa," Sara chimed in, "what about the new initiative I mentioned? I have been thinking it through a bit, but its concept is nowhere near ready for me to bring it up. Maybe I'll use blocked-off time to flesh it out some more. To think about **'What would success look like? What's the ideal end-state? What is the impact we hope it has? What are the key messages I'd need to communicate to get support?'** I could tease out a rough roadmap with milestones along the way. With a habit of regularly blocked-off time, I can really make progress on this."

Melissa smiled. "I love it! You're already using my favourite questions. Also, get yourself in the habit of asking yourself: **What's most important in the moment to get me to the envisioned future**? With this all laid out, you'll feel more confident in your approach and what you're suggesting to others. You can get whatever ideas you might already have swirling around your head into a usable format: a presentation, a brief, talking points, a plan—whatever is the best currency to get you to the next stage. It will be easier to bring others on board with your ideas when there is something a bit more tangible to work with."

Sara replied excitedly, "I can see the possibilities now and for some reason, I'm feeling less overwhelmed. I almost can't wait to get started now."

Melissa then shared with Sara her **Formula for Success: Start. Don't Stop. Modify**.

I know it's a little bit silly to say that this is a formula for success, when it seems so obvious, but the fact is most people just don't start. Or they lose momentum along the way. Or perhaps they don't really reflect on what needs to shift over time. It really does come down to just starting something—not waiting for the perfect time, the perfect conditions, the perfect approach—then not losing energy or attention (and intention). And finally changing it or adjusting it to adapt to what's needed to keep going and to reach the final result. This is especially true when we're talking about new habits, but really it goes for anything we want to accomplish: getting in shape, adopting a new practice, achieving a specific milestone, or spending more time thinking. It all starts with just starting.

It's human nature to get excited and feel motivated in the moment, but then as time goes by, naturally fall back into old patterns. Melissa didn't want to see this happen with Sara. She wanted this excitement to last for her.

Melissa advised Sara to take just a minute or two over the next two weeks to reflect on what was shifting for her—at the end of the day, at the end of a meeting, at the end of the week. As Sara spent time on bigger picture activities as well as on the more day-to-day activities like taking the time to prepare for meetings and such, Melissa encouraged her to ask: **What is the impact of spending that time? What is my energy like?** She told Sara to be honest with herself, though, and notice that every shift, no matter how seemingly insignificant to her, was a step in the right direction and therefore worthy of being called a victory.

"Those little shifts are going to be positive reinforcements. This is where the motivation to keep it up will come from. When you start to see how much more effective you are, how much more intentional you are, you'll be more likely to keep doing it and less likely to give it up," Melissa said.

Sara sat with that advice for a bit and then added, "Well, I'm already motivated about this. By review time, I intend for my higher-ups to notice my ability to lead strategically. There's no way my next review is going to highlight unrealized potential. And I never want to be told I'm not strategic enough again. I'm also motivated since I've already had a powerful experience as mentioned when we started today's session. I felt something shift in me, and I liked it. And everything we've talked about today just feels so much more real—much more aligned to the kind of leader I want to be!"

"That's great, Sara," Melissa commended her. **"So, what will you commit to between now and our next session?"**

Sara committed to scheduling more thinking time this week into her calendar, with plans to fit increasingly more thinking time into the coming weeks. She also decided that some of her thinking time would repeat in her calendar each week. Since her upcoming Thursdays and Fridays were less frantic than the other days of the week, Sara decided she'd start there. She was concerned that when things piled up and the overwhelm started to build, that thinking time would be the first thing to go, but she still committed to putting it in her calendar as a meeting with herself, the same way she would book any other meeting. It would be her time for thinking, planning, and creating, and it needed to be scheduled just as other organization meetings were. Sara realized that this was the way to be intentional and decisive.

"I'll start by starting. I can shift it as needed. But at the end of the week, there's a better chance I can be trusted to 'attend' my own meeting," Sara said with a smile.

> Over time, scheduling time to think and strategize will become such a habit that it will become second nature—a strategic way of doing and being that you can't imagine not doing. And often, a five-minute pause will take you far and might be all you need for many things. You might only need longer time slots for bigger projects, meeting presentations, or change initiatives that you want to propose.

CHAPTER 6

Staying in a Strategic Mindset

Strategic thinking helps to bridge between
where you are and where you want to be.

— *Pearl Zhu*

"Hi, Melissa," Sara said, breezing into the office, appearing a little frazzled. Since their last session, Sara had barely been able to concentrate on anything. A problem had come up about two weeks ago with a very late delivery, an irate buyer, and a supplier who wasn't helping much, and the situation was still unresolved. "I feel like these days are all about damage control," Sara explained. "But they always find a way of working themselves out. We'll get through it." Pausing to catch her breath, Sara said, "It's good to see you again, Melissa."

"You too. And take a deep breath," Melissa said smiling. "I can't wait to hear **what successes you've had since last time—even with all the craziness.**"

Sara took a few more calming breaths and settled into her chair, retracing the past few weeks in her mind. "I wish I could tell you something good, but if I'm to be honest, right now I'm mostly frustrated. I don't think I had any free time this past week for much of anything, not even to break for lunch. And I'm coming here straight from a meeting with my team."

Melissa said, "Shift your thoughts away from that for now. I am certain you had some wins. I'll give you a moment to remember them, even if they feel far away and small at the moment."

There was a long pause. "Hmmm…" Sara slowly grounded herself into the question and said, "Okay, so I'm really digging deep to find a win, and I'm thinking that it might be the few minutes I took to organize my thoughts before going into a senior leader meeting the other day. I think that was a win because it helped me prepare some questions. We ended up talking about a new initiative that I knew nothing about, and it wasn't very clear to me what we were actually trying to do or who would be in charge or why we were considering this initiative. I spoke up and asked, **"What would success look like a year from now?"**

"Absolutely a win!" Melissa congratulated her. "You did something different and not only that, you used exactly what I use with you—a version of my favourite question. What did you notice when you asked that question?"

"Well," Sara answered, "I remembered our sessions and realized it was a good question that probably would benefit others in the room too. And it did! I could feel the energy shift in the room when I asked—almost to one of clarity or relief—more focus, not as frantic or something."

Normally, Sara would have remained quiet in this kind of meeting. She would have tried to figure it out on her own or reprimanded herself for not knowing more about it already or at most, she might have asked a question about the details like the timing. But because she had spent a couple minutes reflecting before the meeting, she was in a different mindset. Her question, which mimicked Melissa's favourite question, helped everyone name the desired impact of the initiative and what it would end up doing in the end. It built alignment about what they were actually trying to do together.

"That's really great! See?" Melissa encouraged her, "Even a few minutes of thinking time can really make a difference and asking a good strategic question like that adds a lot of value!"

"Oh, and another win I guess I can say I had would be the bit of planning I got done on another project that I'm leading," Sara added reflectively, "but that feels like a long time ago now. Even so, it was good to get it done. It will help me adjust some of the other work my team is doing in the next six months."

Melissa smiled again. "I knew you had some successes. Remember, we're looking for shifts in your behaviour and having more impact on a day-to-day basis, even subtle ones. Those sound like good ones. And I'm glad to see you finding wins in what you tell me was a rough few weeks. Now tell me, **what would success look like at the end of our session today?**

Sara sat quietly for several moments. Her mind kept going back to those first pressing questions Melissa asked in their first session: **What kind of leader do I want to be? What impact do I want to have? What do I want to be known for and what type of leader do I want to be?**

She had been journaling almost daily between sessions around those concepts and at this very moment a light went on!

Sara smiled. "This might not answer your question directly about the end of this session, but I know what kind of leader I want to be, and I know what kind of success I want to have. Maybe we can talk about that.

"You asked me once what excites me about all this. You encouraged me to think big. What excites me most is this urge I have to be making a real and meaningful impact by leading on sustainability initiatives. I can see it playing out: it will create value for our organization in terms of revenue, market share, new exciting products, and innovation, but I also want it to be making a real difference by providing products to our customers that are innovative and green. I want us to be leaders in our field on corporate sustainability—both in what products we make, but also in how we make them: our water use, our energy use, the materials we use, our supply chain. We already do this, but I want to lead initiatives that push us to be even better. And I think there are untapped opportunities in product design, how they're transported, how they're reused or disposed of. There is just so much we haven't explored. This is so exciting to me. Meanwhile, I keep getting stuck in the day-to-day operations. I know for sure I'm just too busy doing other things that are needed—I'm not really wasting time, it's all stuff that has to get done. But I'm seeing now how it's limiting me from really leading in the way I really want to on these bigger issues."

Melissa leaned forward enthusiastically. "I love the bigger vision you just described. Not only because I am passionate about these things too, but it has a lot of your values and purpose embedded in there. It's easy to get caught up in your to-do list, or be pulled into meetings or solve problems, but this is where the real transformative change can happen. So, what are some of the things you do to ground yourself back into this bigger picture of you as a successful and impactful leader?"

Sara answered, "I'm not sure if I said this out loud, but I started to journal and I find this to be very helpful. It helps to clarify my thinking. That's one thing I do now."

Melissa asked, "What else did you journal about?"

"Well, I want to be known as a great leader of people, empathetic, supportive, someone who helps others grow and develop and thrive, someone who helps motivate them, so I write about that." Sara paused then added, "Also, I want to be seen as fair. I think I already am, but I'm torn about this one because I think this one also gets me in trouble. I end up getting caught up in helping others too much."

"Well, it's human nature to want to help people," Melissa responded. "And if you feel more comfortable swooping in to help, it becomes your default. It's common to gravitate toward doing what you are comfortable doing and also doing what you know well, what comes easily to you."

Melissa reminded Sara, "You have a lot of empathy and I'm sure it's hard for you to not to do something when you know one of your team members is struggling. Also, you've done many of their jobs when you were at their level before you became a director, so you know what to do and you know what will work. It's natural to want to share that.

"However, you're working twice as much as you need to be because you're probably doing your work and a lot of theirs. To be blunt, when you slip into those patterns, you're being overpaid for what you were hired to do. Of course, that's not exactly true because you're working far more than a regular work week, but I say this to make a point. It is taking you away from work you're supposed to be doing: strategically leading the team and the organization to a vision—to make change and have impact in the ways you just mentioned a few minutes ago. That's why they're paying you at a director level. That's the value you're expected to add. And your team needs that from you too. If you're doing your analysts' or managers' jobs, likely you're not spending as much time or effort on the higher-level strategic stuff. In effect, we always want everyone doing the work at the highest level of their pay grade.

"So, going back to what success looks like, for you to be in a position within the company innovating corporate sustainability, and being a great people leader, **what might you do differently** to put you there, say in two or three years from now?"

"I need to be less involved in the day to day, and I know that up here," Sara said, tapping the side of her head lightly. "Less micromanaging and more time to be creative. I get caught up doing my employees' work and I don't know how to stop so you're right on both counts, Melissa. I end up working twice as much as I need to because I'm essentially doing my job and parts of theirs. And I am not always doing what I'm paid to do, or frankly what is needed for everyone to thrive."

"That's right," Melissa agreed, "and when you're putting your own work aside, you're adding stress that maybe doesn't need to be there. This doesn't mean you have to stop helping your people. It probably means that it's time to look at how you might 'help' differently and what value you can provide to them. In effect, it's being *strategic* in *how* you help them. And maybe help isn't even the best word. Maybe it's something like enable or empower or motivate or engage or oversee or lead—there are lots of other words that might have a bit different energy and intent. We want to find new ways for you to lead them so in essence, when you're operating at your highest level, you're providing more opportunities for your team members to exercise their own potential AND you're adding the most value to the organization. Make sense?"

"Makes sense," Sara said. She couldn't disagree with that.

Melissa continued exploring with Sara what it means to be a more strategic leader. She offered some other questions to consider. **What do you want your reputation to be?** We sometimes call this your brand. In thinking this through, ask yourself, **What do you want your higher ups to be saying about you behind your back? What do you want to be known for? What types of projects or meetings do you want them to think of you for and invite you to? Five years from now, what do you want to have accomplished?** These are all questions that help you define that a bit more.

As she listened, Sara's wheels were turning. She knew that she wanted to be known as an asset. Someone with vision who is creative and innovative. To be known for her passion about sustainability, and Sara knew that at the end of her career, that's where she'd like to leave her mark. To be seen as someone who effectively leads these initiatives, not just manages them, or solves problems.

She came out of her reverie and said, "I truly want to make a difference in this industry and for this company. I want them to allow me to create programs that support sustainability within our infrastructure and to see these qualities in me. But you know what, Melissa? Now I know I keep repeating this, but these days, I'm just so overwhelmed by day-to-day interactions and problem solving within my department and that's not winning me any points with my higher ups. I'm certainly not making any meaningful changes."

"Well, this is a good place for us to start," Melissa reiterated. "You can see what success looks like for you but right now, you're feeling trapped in the doing and reacting. Email notifications ding in and you're on it. Deadlines approach, you're hyper-focused on that. Someone has a question, you drop everything. Someone needs help with a problem, you step right into the problem. Am I right that these are the kinds of things winning your attention and your time and stealing you from your own vision within your career?"

Sara sighed with a hearty but frustrated, "Yes."

"There are a lot of different pieces to being strategic. On the people side of things, there are plenty of renowned, influential leaders who are also empathetic and care deeply about people. How do they do it? They are strategic about it."

Melissa continued, "We've already established that you care deeply about people, so it makes sense that your first inclination is to swoop in and make it easy for them. You do this most for your direct reports, but it sounds like you do this with others too: when a peer asks you for something or your boss requests something urgent. We want to change your default of getting caught up in the day-to-day minutiae and in doing a lot of the work for your team or others. We want to get you to start moving towards where you want to be."

Sara felt a little defensive and explained, "I recognize that sometimes I need to delegate a bit more, but I see how much work they have, and I know a lot of them are working really late and I don't want to add more to their plate. And a lot of times it's just faster for me to do it myself. It's hard for me to know how to delegate when I see how busy they are."

"You're protecting them, which is, in theory, admirable, but it's not helping them grow," Melissa said. "Let me ask you to think about it this way: Where did the most growth in your own career come from? From being rescued or being supported?"

"It definitely was when I was challenged with something I was excited about but maybe was a bit scary. Or when my boss was too busy and let me take the lead on something. I was so proud of myself when I did well in those instances." Sara acquiesced, "And, okay, I can hear myself saying exactly what you're probably getting me to realize. I see the parallels. And even if I was busy, I'm sure I would have been more upset to not have had the opportunity to push myself, to grow, to evolve."

Melissa took it deeper. "Every time someone needs you and you dive right into solving their problem, you're taking away from their potential to do more and grow. And every bit of time that you spend executing on somebody else's work is time you're probably putting off from doing the strategic stuff. So, there are a few dynamics happening here."

Sara began to see it from this new perspective. She wanted her people to have opportunities but maybe she was making assumptions about what she thought they can handle, without giving them a fair shot to show what they were capable of. Maybe her automatic response to jump in and help wasn't helping them grow and also was derailing her from her bigger vision for herself.

"I'm beginning to see this more clearly now," Sara admitted. "And also, there's another thing I'm starting to realize too. I can't believe I'm going to say this out loud now but…well, I'm here to be coached so I might as well be fully transparent. If I'm to be honest, Melissa, when I sit down to do strategic work, it doesn't feel productive. When I sense the commotion of people all over the place getting things done it makes me feel irresponsible to just sit, think and plan—like I'm not pulling my weight, or not contributing. So, when I'm actively contributing when things are busy, at least it feels like I'm doing something and helping us accomplish what needs to get done."

Melissa smiled. "What you just said is a huge revelation. I see this quite often, but it usually takes people a bit longer to come to that realization. **It requires a different energy to**

think strategically than to execute. Being strategic doesn't have that adrenaline rush that getting through a busy day checking things off your list does. And for "doers" like yourself who were promoted for their abilities to get stuff done, it feels out of sync. But the reality is the company is paying you to be strategic at your level, which involves spending time doing the forward-thinking and planning. And the execution part will benefit from this too. Without a doubt! It just won't be you doing it. Or at least not as much, or maybe you are doing something slightly different."

"Well, I'm also thinking that maybe my default is set to do what feels comfortable," Sara added, "the work I had done for years before stepping into my role as a director. It comes easy to me, and I feel like I'm accomplishing more because I'm accomplishing something—granted, I see now they aren't really my things, but you know... sometimes it's harder to do some of the strategic thinking..."

Melissa agreed. "It is harder much of the time to do the strategic thinking until you shift into new thinking patterns and mindsets. So, let's recap your patterns: you're protecting your people by doing their work so you don't overwhelm them, and you're also doing work that probably should be done by them because it's a little bit easier or it's something you know how to do because you've done it before, or maybe even simply because you like to do it or you get more satisfaction from it. There's also a piece that also comes up for many people that their work is probably something you can check off or complete, whereas a lot of strategic work doesn't have that same sense of completion or closure."

Sara nodded, and Melissa continued. "But ideally, we want to spend time on what adds the most value over the long term, and helps other people succeed, which in your case is to be spending some of that time planning and thinking and visioning and all the other stuff we've talked about. Everyone in the organization has a specific value to add and yours is now more in being strategic and in enabling others to succeed and much less in day-to-day delivering."

"Yeah," Sara responded, "but if someone comes to me asking how to do something, I still want to help them."

"Of course you're going to help them!" Melissa assured Sara. "I just want you to be more strategic in *how* you help. That's what we're going to dive into right now."

When you execute on someone else's behalf, doing work that is theirs, it's as if their work becomes yours. You end up taking ownership even if you don't intend to or realize it. If you want to keep the accountability with them, you can become more like an advisor or even better, an enabler, because an advisor implies that we're telling people what to do and that's only somewhat better than doing it for them. Ideally you want to help people figure it out on their own and in so doing, keep the power and accountability with them.

Melissa then gave Sara some actions she could take.

"When someone asks you a question," Melissa began, "answer it with a question. Or many questions. And the questions you're going to use are *what* questions, not why and how questions.

What questions tend to open conversations and open their thinking.

- **What would success look like?**
- **What's important about that?**
- **What's the purpose?**
- **What are the benefits?**
- **What's the impact?**
- **What's the desired future?**
- **What's the ideal end-state?**
- **What's the best-case scenario?**

Those are opening, future-focused, strategic questions that create a vision and purpose even if it's for something small, they open dialogue, and they develop critical thinking."

Why and *How* questions tend to narrow conversations. *Why* and *How* questions are perfectly good questions when we're analyzing content or details.

For instance, a *Why* question is great to narrow down to identify a root cause. You may have heard the concept of digging deeper with the five "whys" to get to the cause and effect of things. *Why* questions are great if you're trying to understand a circumstance, understand the content. In general,

Why questions are very useful. However, they are just not as good when it's directed *at* an individual. In essence, a *Why* question invites the person to justify their position which causes them to focus on that issue, narrow their thinking and maybe even dig their heels in a bit. It can also inadvertently cause defensiveness in a person. And sometimes it can feel like an interrogation. You just need to understand the unintended impact when it's directed at someone, and you typically get a bit less than that with a *What* question.

Likewise, *How* questions put people into their analytical brain, which is, again, not necessarily bad, but if you're trying to get them to think more creatively about something or to open their thinking a *How* question might not be as effective as a *What* question especially if you ask it too early. *How* questions also narrow you to a solution, which can be useful, but often they are used a bit too soon in the process before the creative thinking of what's possible has happened.

For both *Why* and *How* questions, you can reframe the same question into a "what": For instance: instead of asking "*Why* did you do it that way?" ask "**What led to that decision or approach?**" Instead of asking "How will you do this?" ask "**What are the three next steps that will get us close to our desired end-state**". These may seem like subtle differences, but they do matter.

"I love *What* questions. You'll notice I mostly use *What* questions in coaching. I ask questions that start with the word "what" and tend to be bigger-picture and more future-focused. *What* questions typically open up the mind and the conversation. *What* questions help you define what's important, and what the future desired end-state could be. That gives us a direction to head in. All questions are valuable, of course; they just have a different impact on how they are received.

"So, from now on, when somebody comes to you and asks you how to do something, instead of telling them right away, follow up with a few *What* questions.

- **What have you tried so far?**
- **What were you thinking of trying?**
- **What would success look like in the ideal end state?**
- **What are you hoping this looks like when we're done?**
- **What are some benefits you're trying to gain?**

"It's not to say you can never use other questions – in fact, "who" or "when" questions are highly valuable. And "how" and "why" questions are good too in certain circumstances or certain timing. I just want you to practice the 'what' questions for now.

"So, with all of this, you're still supporting them to get something done, but you are also helping them develop their critical thinking, so your questions not only prompt them in the moment, but they are questions that teach them how to think about it."

Sara scribbled some notes while Melissa explained all this to her and then leaned back in her chair to absorb it all.

"It feels weird to start being different with them. How can I put this into practice without throwing them off?" she asked. "For example, just yesterday my account manager asked me how to start a project he was assigned to lead. I jumped right in and told him what to do, who to contact, where to start. I even said I'd write the project charter when he wasn't sure what to do and said I'd reach out to two colleagues in the organization to get some answers for him. If I could go back and do it over again, can you play out the scene for me? **What would have been a more strategic way to handle it?**"

Melissa smiled. "I'm happy to provide some suggestions, but let's start with your perspective: **What would have been a more effective approach**?

"Ha-ha, you're doing it to me, aren't you?" Sara chuckled. "Well, I'd start by asking the four or five *What* questions we mentioned a few minutes ago. I want to keep the ownership and accountability with them. Teach a man to fish and all that?"

"Yup!" Melissa nodded enthusiastically.

Listening is more of a passive activity. When you tell people what to do, they're not fully engaged, even if they're trying to be. Whereas, when you ask them a question, they have to interpret the question, think about it, formulate a response, and then speak to it. This is much more engaging than just listening. And questions help people develop their own critical thinking about the issue.

But then Sara wondered, "And what happens if they don't know what to do at all? If it's brand new?"

Melissa smiled, "**What might work here?** You tell me."

Sara played along. "I can feel how my own struggle with this is making me learn just by you asking me. Point taken! So maybe if I give them some suggestions, I could follow up with a couple questions. Like "**What's the purpose of this project – what will it be used for?**" Or, "**What would you want it to do at the end?**" "**What would it look like if it all worked out?**" Or, "**What about this really resonates with how you want to proceed?**" Or "**What other stakeholders should be engaged at this step?**" Or even, "**What are the first three things you'll do?**" Or "**What will you try by the end of the week?**"

"Now you're getting the hang of it! What's that like now that you've named some of the questions you might have used?"

Having fun with it, Sara continued, "Gosh, now that I'm attuned to your questions, I see how many you really ask like this. And it's really good. It makes me better at thinking about things–to think about them strategically!

"But to answer your question, I'm actually kind of excited about it. Not only can I see how this would help them think about this better, but I'm also noticing that these same questions would help me in my own projects. I don't always think through these bigger questions before I jump in and just start just doing things.

"I think I might be more comfortable with all this if I could give them a heads up that I'll be shifting how I answer their questions or requests and give them reasons or context as to why I'm doing this. I want them to know that I'm asking questions to develop not only myself but them as well. To develop their autonomy and such… Otherwise, it might seem weird that all of sudden I'm trying new tactics on them instead of my usual jumping in and doing it for them."

"By all means, absolutely," Melissa agreed. "Be transparent. You might say, 'As I develop my own leadership, I'm going to actually focus on developing yours too and this is part of that.' You could even link it to any career aspirations they might have articulated and demonstrate how this will set them up for better opportunities.

"Just know that you might get some subtle or unconscious resistance when you start asking questions instead of just giving answers or doing it for them, because they're used to it being easier. If they are used to you taking up the slack, and you're no longer doing this, or if you're nudging them into areas that feel a little uncomfortable because they haven't done it before, they might unconsciously resist. It might feel frustrating to them that they have to struggle a bit."

"Yeah, like I did with you just a few minutes ago," Sara said. She had wanted Melissa to give her the answer, but she got so much more out of it by saying the questions out loud herself. "I'll remember them more and now they flow just a little bit better out of my mouth."

"You've got it," Melissa said, encouraging Sara to keep going with it. "It'll sort itself out, especially because they already know that you have their best interests at heart. I have no doubt that you'll do this in a supportive way."

As you step back from swooping in to save the day and take over work your people are meant to do, another piece is to be clear about what role you want to play for them. This is a useful approach for interactions of many kinds. Let's say someone comes into your office with an issue or problem, or you're on a call with a customer or in a meeting with your higher ups—whatever the scenario, someone needs something from you. You can start by asking them directly what they are expecting to get from you. You can say something like this... "I want to make sure I'm helping you in the best way, or providing the most value to you: what role do you want me to play here? Are you looking for help in making a decision, or to brainstorm some ideas? Are you looking for a sounding board or for approval?"

People might not know the answer to this right away, because they probably haven't thought about it, but the more we ask these types of questions of people, the clearer they will be about what they are wanting from you. It's unlikely they're going to come in and say, "Well I actually want you to do my work for me." When you do this, you're forcing their hand a bit to think about what they're actually wanting from you, and this allows you to stay at the highest level that you can support them in.

"And so Sara, these are the pieces of the puzzle to be more strategic in how you interact with people, especially your team, but also with anyone really," Melissa said, starting to wrap up this week's session. "It's going to happen gradually, with subtle and yet profound changes: in how you will be perceived, in shifts in how you think and work on your initiatives and your goals, and in their abilities to perform. As you build on this strategy, your natural inclination to respond by taking ownership of their work will be replaced with you leading more strategically and you will see their own abilities to think critically and resolve problems improve. They will come to you less and when they do, they will already have some inkling of the kinds of questions to expect from you.

"In terms of actions, I'd like you to come up with four or five questions that you will ask before giving answers. This will help you be ready to answer their question with a question. We've already come up with many today, and there are others you could adopt, too. Just pick a few for now and try them. I don't want you to be overwhelmed with the choices. Remember, the key is to start," Melissa said with a smile.

"And if they truly don't know how to proceed, or they only seem to be able to answer part of the solution, you can brainstorm with them, that's fine. Just follow up with additional questions after that. Be careful of asking questions that have a yes/no answer, or questions that are statements just in the form of a question like, 'You'd start by speaking with Operations, wouldn't you?' Instead, let's say they say something like: 'Well, I think maybe someone in finance would be a good place to start and maybe the HR committee that deals with this'. You could say, 'Yes, those sound great. **Who specifically would you reach out to? And what about operations? What's the impact this project will have on operations? Who else could you reach out to?**' And then together you might decide who are the right people for them to reach out to in that scenario.

"Or they might tell you some ideas about how they want to proceed, and you add: 'That sounds good. **What about the risks – what have you considered so far?** or 'Based on what we just discussed, **What will you try first?**' or **What have you tried so far?**' **I just suggested a model to consider, what do you know about that?** or 'What projects have we done that are similar to this?' Or 'What methodology might work in this situation?' or 'What don't you know that you still need to find out?'** So even though you've given them ideas, you're keeping the ownership with them.

"These are just some ideas. Make them natural, of course. You could even tell them upfront that you're going to ask them a few questions to help them frame their thought process. I know you'll do this, but make the questions feel curious and collaborative rather than it feel like you're drilling them. And have fun with it! Notice the impact when you ask questions versus telling the answers."

"Sounds good, Melissa. Thank you." Sara closed her notebook, and as she began to rise, Melissa asked her, **"What else will you commit to doing?"**

"I'm going to ask more 'what' questions instead of jumping in to solve problems for others. I'm going to write out my boldest ideas of what kind of company we *could* be related to sustainability initiatives. And I'm going to keep envisioning my growth as a leader of impact within this organization. It's going to happen!"

CHAPTER 7

What Do My Higher-Ups Care About?

"To be native to a place we must learn to speak its language."
— *Robin Wall Kimmerer*

Flipping through some notes, Melissa was looking for where she and Sara left off in the last session and when she found what she was looking for asked, "Ahhh, yes, Sara, so how did it go with your direct reports in the past few weeks? Did you have a chance to try something new with them?"

Sara was really excited to talk about it. She had tried something new, and in the process, Sara learned something new about herself. Sara realized that when she had the answers to people's questions or requests, it made her feel smart. It gave her a sense of power, and her ego had a blast. But then a little over a week ago, three times with three different direct reports, she used the 'answer-a-question-with-a-question' strategy, and it showed her something so profound it blew her away. Sara realized that she could have more of a positive influence by *not* giving answers. This showed her the tremendous power in not having to provide all the answers. And it also energized her. For the first time she knew what it felt like to not get bogged down in figuring out other people's stuff. Add to that, Sara loved witnessing them as they grew more engaged, more confident, and more excited, creating an all-around much more dynamic interaction.

Sara told Melissa that just this week she had been in the position to hand the authority back to three of her people, and not only did they do very well with the exchange, they got what they needed done—without her diving right in.

"Anyway," Sara exclaimed, "I couldn't wait to tell you how great I feel about it. It feels easy and I see the benefits of this new strategy. It's going to end up saving me a lot of time and energy from doing work that isn't mine to do. And I already see that they're going to gain more autonomy and confidence."

The best way to change the course of outcomes is by breaking the patterns that keep repeating the same outcomes. When you have a tendency to jump right in with answers or to find ways to make it quick and easy for others, it is your own time and energy being spent. Sometimes you're not even aware that you're making it easy for people to ask you instead of figuring it out themselves. It's not intentional. It's just a pattern you've both unconsciously fallen into.

It often seems like quick fixes will save time, but in the long run, nurturing your people's innate abilities to handle their jobs with your guidance is going to be a multi-way win. They become less dependent on you and grow more into their potential. You become better at guiding them, which is more strategic and is the reason you're in the position you're in. And you can choose to pay attention to your own work and your own priorities. And the organization gets the best out of everyone because you're all doing more of what you are hired to do.

"Well," Melissa jumped in. "Clearly, if I asked what success looked like for you last week, this would have to be it! I'm so happy for you."

"Yes, thank you," Sara said. "This strategy works beautifully, and I feel really good about it!"

"Great. So, what's on your mind for today?" Melissa asked. **"What would success look like at the end of our session?"**

"Well, I have a board presentation coming up on Friday that I prepared for." Sara then added, "There are some kinks to work out and I'm waiting for more information to add to the presentation deck. I guess success today would be me feeling more prepared about this and feeling confident that I'm communicating the right messages."

"You know my first question," Melissa challenged Sara, **"What would success look like leaving that board meeting on Friday?"**

Sara groaned, pushing back into her chair with a deep sigh. *I should have seen that question coming,* she thought. *Okay, Sara, think . . .* **what would success look like** *after leaving Friday's meeting?*

"I want to feel that I provided value," she finally said, "and that I didn't mess up. I want them to think that I know what I'm talking about."

Melissa loved that Sara was thinking about these things before the session. Melissa also wanted to make sure that Sara was preparing and thinking about the most important aspects, so she asked Sara what she was spending her time thinking about to prepare.

> In anticipation of the meeting that was coming up, Sara made sure she had all the data to show where they were at in the project plan. She wanted to be sure she had the causes and explanations for some of the delays. And she wanted to feel confident that she could discuss the financial targets and analytics. She wanted to show what her group had done so far and be ready for any questions they might have. Well before the meeting, Sara analyzed the data they had collected, she prepared several graphs with that data, she updated the timelines, and she also prepared answers to some of the questions that she thought could come up about the project.
>
> She did all the necessary and useful prep work. She had what she needed to cover all the background information. But did Sara also think about how she would present this to the members at this meeting? **Who would be around the table? What did the leaders at that level care about?** Did they care about the details of the project? Or did they have more of an interest in not meeting with any surprises if something was off-track? Would they want to know about risks that may arise? Would Sara present at the level that they cared about?

Instead of going into the details of the project, Sara will likely want to talk high-level about some of those things. Some of the questions that her higher ups will likely want to know about:

- **At a high-level, how is everything tracking related to the deadlines and milestones?**
- **What risks should they be aware of?**
- **What are the three most important things for them to know?**

Sara's boss likes when she shows him everything, so she prepared a PowerPoint with extensive particulars about the project, making sure not to leave anything out. She figured that if she covered all the bases, she would make sure something would hit home with everyone there. But was there something more to think about before going into this meeting, with this group of people? Did Sara's boss's boss really care about every little detail? And did the others want to sift through what they don't care about to get to what they're looking for?

What should Sara do? Should she scrap everything she did?

Not at all. If it makes her feel more confident to prepare by considering all the details, then she should do that. In fact, she probably needs to go through some of it herself when she's preparing for the meeting in order to know the background and wrap her head around what's important.

But if it's not something the people in the room care about, it would be best to leave it out of the actual presentation. A presentation to the board should be direct and to the point: short, simple, substantiated, persuasive, factual, and honest. The board members don't have the time or headspace for a slew of slides with information they don't care about.

"You said that you want people at the board meeting to see that you know what you're talking about," Melissa repeated. "And you want to know that you provided value, right?"

Yes, exactly," Sara reaffirmed.

"Make a mental note of this," Melissa said. "Think at least two levels up. Think about what your boss's boss Margo cares about. What kind of questions will she have? When Margo was in the room at past presentations, what did she and the others who were there brush off? **What did the board members ask about?** Where did they seem distracted or even impatient? **What did they focus on? What questions did they ask you or others in the meeting?** They're waiting to hear answers to the things they care about…"

"What does someone two levels up from you care about?" is a great question to reflect upon, or even ask others about, and not just for these types of meetings, but often. Even in your day-to-day, **What does your boss' boss think about, care about, worry about, talk about? What keeps her (and her peers) up at night?** These questions (even to yourself) will help redirect you when you're too much in the details or the weeds of delivery. Your boss' perspective matters too, of course, but this two-levels up concept is just a little bit more meta-view.

Just to give Sara some examples, Melissa explained that boards generally watch over the long-term value, impact, and risks. They might be looking at growth and sustainability of the company. If the organization has a focus on leading social issues, they might care about how your project fits into those issues. "You will want to talk about the kinds of things people two levels up care about and what they value. You might be guessing a bit. It could be that everyone cares about different things. Maybe Margo wants to know about contribution to society, and someone else might ask about profitability. Someone else might care about the risks to a new area of the business. Others might want to know about competitors. You want to find out what matters to them and build your narrative around that.

"If you've been invited to the meeting to present something to them – some, if not all– are already warm to the project. So, what are they thinking about and what are they looking for from you? Get right into what matters to them.

"Let this sink in: The presentation is less about the project and more about the implications of the project. What impact will it have at the organizational level, at the industry level, at the finance level, at the environmental, at the social impact level—depending on who's in the room when you present?"

Trying to absorb it all, Sara asked, "How can I know what matters to them if I don't know them personally?"

"That's the trickiest part," Melissa admitted. "Some of that comes from observing them and noticing what they pay attention to, what questions they ask. Some might come from discussion with your boss or your peers or others in the organization about what they generally ask about and care about. And a lot of it will be just guessing what you think matters to them. You won't always get it right, but the fact that you're thinking about this at all means you'll get closer to it being what resonates with them. It's not only about getting the right answers to these questions, it's expanding your thinking into their perspective.

"Basically, you want to look at the meta-view of the project. Think about what their meetings are likely to cover.

- **What do they talk about?**
- **Who do they meet with?**
- **What do they worry about?**
- **What does a typical day in their meetings look like?**
- **What do they care about?**
- **What do they obsess about?**
- **What other stakeholders do they have to think about: shareholders, investors, customers, potential new customers, competitors?**

"Here are some other things to consider when you're thinking about your project:

- **What's the impact of this project to the business?**
- **What's the connection to other projects that might be happening or other initiatives?**

- **What's the connection to the organizational goals, its mission, its values?**

"These are the types of questions that you want to be thinking about when you're preparing the presentation. In general, as a director, you often need to be thinking about what your Senior VP cares about (or higher for certain projects or situations). Do you really need 29 slides with every detail of the project? Does your Senior VP need or care about all that? In this case, you need to think also about what the board cares about. In all cases, they're busy people looking at the business as a whole. Your boss' boss has a broader view than you have; she has more insight into other areas of the business."

At this point in the coaching, Sara chimed in, "So I'm thinking of that expression, 'can't see the forest for the trees?' You're saying I shouldn't look at the trees."

"Well, it's probably more that you should look at the trees from the view of a helicopter overlooking the forest," Melissa explained further. "The details are important, and they want to know that *you* are looking out for all the details *as well as* the meta-view when you're leading your team. But what *they* want to know is: **What's important about what you're seeing?** Your job is to interpret what you're seeing in the details and make some sense of it on their behalf.

"The two levels up person – whether it's your boss's boss Margo or anyone else for that matter—is probably thinking about what they're going to say at their board meeting or their next shareholder meeting. Or perhaps they're looking at where to make some longer-term investments in their operations. Or looking at the trends in their customer needs. Or a whole host of other things. Using the idea of '**What does someone two levels up care about?**' is just to get you to look at what's important at a higher level than you and often your boss' perspective is just a bit too close. Many leaders are strategic about a particular project but not strategic from a higher level or seeing how it fits into the business. This is just a simple way to help you get to the bigger picture. In this case, we're also specifically looking at what the board cares about, which is even a higher-level view than your Senior VP."

At this point Melissa was met with a little resistance from Sara. "I get it. I do. And it makes sense. I'm just still a bit reluctant to give up all the work my team and I already did. We put a lot into these presentations, and it's still odd to me that no one wants to know."

Melissa reassured her, "It's not that no one wants to know. It might have been important for you and your team to delve into that level of detail. It might have helped you make sense of the meta-view. Or maybe it wasn't. But regardless, remember, your role in this upcoming meeting is to present the most important information in the most concise and clear way to these very busy people to help them make decisions, and run the business.

"So I'll ask again, "**What would success look like on Friday? What impact do you want to have?**"

"I guess it's exactly that: to help them run with business and make good decisions," Sara answered.

"And here's more for you to think about," Melissa pressed on. **"What would success look like for <u>how</u> you show up?** This is the *be* part we've talked about before. And, **what do you want them to say about your presentation (and you) if they were talking after the meeting?"**

"Hmmm…" Sara paused to think about this. "Well, I want them to think I've added strategic value, that I've provided the best insight possible into what's important to them and not wasted their time. I'd like someone in the room to walk away thinking, *This director really gets it!*"

Melissa gave Sara two-thumbs up. "Exactly. So it's *not* about you being the expert—or not exactly anyway. It's about you being almost like a strategic advisor for the work you're leading. Can you see how that shifts the way you approach the upcoming presentation on Friday? And the way it can also change the energy you bring to the room?"

"Well," Sara said, "there's still a small part of me that feels like maybe they won't think I'm smart or they won't think I know enough or something."

"A lot of people hold on to beliefs like that, and it's easy for that kind of thinking to get in the way of a strategy that is necessary to grasp," Melissa responded. She told Sara the following story that illustrates how over-presenting is such a common derailer, particularly when insecurity influences someone to over-deliver.

A senior manager client in a huge company was looking to be promoted to a director. The move up in that company was the equivalent of Director to VP in Sara's company. It was quite a senior position and the first level of executive. This man had been on their high-potential list for four or five years, but he never got promoted. He was always told he wasn't strategic enough, especially in his presentations, but he wasn't quite sure what that meant. When he gave board presentations, he came very prepared. His previous presentation had 67 slides, and he believed every slide was important. Well, after one or two sessions with Melissa, he was down to one slide. One! Melissa and this client hadn't even finished working together and he was already settling into his new position as Director. He was promoted within two or three months after they started working together. It finally clicked for him to focus on what was important to the others in the room.

"Wait just a minute!" Sara said in amazement. "How is a one-slide presentation even possible?"

Melissa explained, "Well, it won't always be enough. But in this case, he tapped into the core of what the seven or however many higher-ups who were in the boardroom cared about and presented on that."

"That's a serious reframe," Sara tried to wrap her head around it. "Wouldn't one little slide make me look like I rushed the job or didn't care? How would I even know what not to prepare, or what not to bring?"

"Before you go into a board meeting, know who's there and what they're there to accomplish at the meeting. It could be all they care about is costs, timelines, and risks. Or maybe you're presenting to higher ups who right now are concerned about social impact, innovation, and growth. Think about how bored they'll be sitting through 67 slides of stuff they don't care about. In fact, they wouldn't likely even let you get past two slides—they'd probably interrupt you to ask the questions they really cared about. Now, imagine hitting all the marks in a clear concise manner.

The bottom line is: don't show up to an executive board meeting with 67 slides. Or 33 or sometimes not even 10. Really. You just don't. Maybe you have 10+ slides because you feel better prepared and you need them for your confidence, but you don't necessarily show them all. You can pull them up depending on the questions you get instead of going through them one-by-one, but don't present them unless it makes sense or unless someone asks. Sometimes it makes sense to prepare a few extra slides that you might use if they ask for more clarification, or if they ask certain questions. You come across as ready. It shows you've anticipated their questions. And it gives you confidence too, because you know you have it if you need it. So, I've given these specific number of slides as a demonstration of what I'm talking about; there is no rule, and of course there are times when more slides are needed or you're running a full day meeting, or some meetings require a detailed look at something specific, or some senior executives like more details and background, or whatever. I'm just saying to be very *intentional* about the number of slides and what you put on those slides for your main presentation, and have back-up slides where needed.

"Often it is appropriate to send materials you want them to review ahead of time–those materials could have more background detail if you think it's useful. Boards don't like to be surprised and some individuals like to take their time reviewing the information. But in person: present on a handful, or less than a handful."

Melissa finished explaining this strategy and then asked Sara, "**What would success look like when presenting to your senior executives? What shift in mindset would help you out here?**"

"In the past," Sara answered, "presenting projects to the board has always been 'what details do I need to show?' When I feel that I do that well, I feel like I succeeded. I'm trying to absorb this idea now that I must redirect my thinking away from the project details and towards '**What do they care about?**'

"That's for the presentation, but overall, I also need to shift my mindset away from task-oriented successes to '**What impact do I want to have?**' or '**What do I want to influence?**' and go after that. I'm starting to see with all this coaching we're doing that to become more strategic in the way I lead is to change what I think about and the way I think and that will reflect in what I do…"

"Yes," Melissa nodded in agreement. "You're presenting in their perspective and in their reality. That's why I say observe people in the board meeting when you're there. **Who's talking about what, who's asking what kinds of questions, who gets**

excited about what? Getting the pulse on this is part of the strategic thinking process that will help you know what they want from you."

It was becoming clear to Sara that if she felt better preparing all the details of the project, she could still go through the process of preparing more than is needed. It's still okay to do that. It's just not okay to show it all unless it's needed or asked for. Just like the client story Melissa shared earlier, it may be only a handful of slides or less. Still, Sara was struggling with how. "How," she wondered, "will I be able to do that? For example, this presentation we're talking about for the Friday meeting is 24 slides."

Melissa assured her it was doable. "You can do it by following the clues. They're all around you. For example, when you're at the board meetings, **What is Margo saying? What questions does she ask?** If you can sense the kinds of questions she asks, you can plan your presentation with her concerns already accounted for before she has a chance to ask. Also, when you're there, observe the others. **What do they do, where's the most controversy, where do they get stuck, what are the dynamics?** In these meetings, **at what critical points do you see higher ups turning 'no' into a 'yes'?**"

Sara chuckled as she told Melissa about the many meetings she'd sat through where she scanned a room, observing other people. Often, she had the sense that everyone was in their own little bubbles, just kind of waiting for the meeting to end so they could get back to working.

Melissa smiled and said, "That's the switch. If people seem bored, preoccupied, like their mind is somewhere else, they're not using the time at the meeting to be there fully, to be present with the others, in a strategic sense. The most strategically thinking people at the table are watching and listening and they're aware of everything going on around them. They're looking for the clues, **who seems to care about and what and who contributes what** and they're storing the information to be used at some later time or meeting. There is so much gold in simply observing and listening.

"You could also reflect on or look at their professional backgrounds. Those with a finance background will definitely come with that mindset: budgets, return on investment, financial risk, etc. In fact, financials *are* a big part of what most executives obsess about. Human Resource professionals will be looking at resources, training, retention — stuff like that. Someone spearheading social issues or community outreach will want to understand things from that lens. You might be able to look at board meeting minutes, or at least ask your boss Aaron about what the board cares about—that often drives senior executives too.

"Look at the company vision and strategy — what clues do you get from that? **Where are most of your corporate initiatives focused these days: growth, long-term sustainability, social issues, new products?** You could ask peers who have presented to them too. And as you get more comfortable with the dynamic, you're going to start to see patterns. Some boards, and some senior executive teams do like a lot more detail than others. So you'll have to adapt. If you're ready with your background information, you'll be able to address it. But start presenting at a high-level and layer down to specific details as needed."

Actions you can take to gain insight into what matters most to the higher-ups:

- Ask for a skip-level meeting once a month, once a quarter or whatever seems reasonable in your organization. This is a meeting with your boss' boss. It's pretty common in many organizations. Likewise, it's good to do the same with your direct reports' direct reports.
- Notice what questions your boss' boss asks in meetings, or what they linger on, or what they make statements about.
- Ask your boss (or your boss' boss) if it's appropriate for you to sit in on and/or participate in parts of certain strategic meetings; or perhaps ask questions about them before and after the fact.
- Seek to understand how your individual and team goals feed up to your boss and your boss' boss goals.
- Set up intentional and regular meetings with peers who have the same boss' boss; share stories, observations, learnings about what might be important to him/her.

Melissa went on to say, "Peer relationships are very underutilized in most organizations. Understanding your peers, their challenges, their focus, and their vision for their areas of responsibility enhances your ability to see what is important across the organization. Sometimes their priorities can strengthen your efforts, but at other times their priorities can compete with yours—for resources, for attention, for funding. Your peers all feed up to people more senior to you. Developing good allies and collaboration with your peers will improve your strategic understanding of the direction of the organization."

Sara listened intently, absorbing it all, and then said, "I understand how this thinking strategically could be game changing for me. And yet, it still feels a little overwhelming. I'm sure you're going to give me homework on this."

"Of course!" Melissa smiled. "**What will you commit to following this discussion?**"

Sara took a few seconds then said, "I'm going to think through a lot of the questions we discussed today, set a frame for what I think is most important and prepare my presentation that way. I'll go through my thinking with my boss and maybe two peers that I don't work with much but who I know present a lot to these same people and get their perspective on what this group cares about. And I have an informal mentor in another area of the business. I'm going to ask what she thinks too. I'll prepare some additional slides as back-up but they'll be more on-demand or as I think they're needed.

"I'm a bit nervous, but I'm also a bit excited about this. I can feel how this will add more value. And, of course, I'm going to practice.

"And, I'm going to dig into **what value do I want to add** and **how do I want to show up in this meeting**. It will be a shift for me to be seen in this more strategic way, but I like it."

In wrapping up this week's session, Melissa re-emphasized how this approach really does add more value. She let Sara know that reaching out to her peers for this was a great idea since peers are the most underutilized resource in organizations. Leaders often reach out to their peers for their content expertise, but rarely for leadership or management insight. Peers will experience some of the same challenges you have and also know some of the same dynamics you're looking for. You can share your impressions, assumptions, and experience about the senior leadership to better anticipate what's necessary. You can share successes and mishaps to learn from each other.

In an earlier session Sara mentioned that her boss encouraged her to interact with her peers more often, so before ending this session, Melissa encouraged Sara to incorporate more frequent interactions with her peers, reminding her that the insight gained is invaluable. Intentional connecting and engaging with peers typically increases your ability to influence, and gives insight into other areas you don't normally see. Continuing to do this over time helps you to make better decisions and create better visions, strategies, and plans than when working siloed.

Before saying goodbye, Melissa reminded Sara, "I know you have it in you to knock this out of the park. You're good at being prepared for important things: you're just going to be prepared in a different way. In our conversations you're already definitely looking at these things more from these bigger picture perspectives. Remember, it's not about you, so don't get caught up in your head or worried about how you are coming across. It's about you giving them the best insight. And you were put in this role because you have that to offer."

CHAPTER 8

Focusing on the Big Rocks

*Everybody has a role to play in making our communities
work well. The roles are very different but equally important in
terms of ensuring the community functions the way it should.*
                                            — *Jodi Wilson-Raybould*

Sara had been putting the new strategies into place. She came into
this week's session feeling really good about her progress, and she
was especially excited to talk about her successes related to the
board presentation. It went great! She felt much more ready and
capable even though she was a bit nervous. She walked out of the
meeting feeling she gave them most of what they were looking for.

There are a few things she would have done differently, but
luckily her intentional preparation meant she was able to address
their concerns pretty quickly and stay focused on important
messages and themes. She told Melissa that after her presentation
when she could relax a bit more and observe the people and
dynamics around her, she did observe each of the board members
and senior leadership team, asking herself the following questions:

- **What's his angle?**
- **What's important to her?**

- **What kind of questions do each of them ask and what's likely behind those questions?**
- **What are each of them worried about or focused on?**
- **What do each of them want for this organization?**

She didn't have all the answers, of course, but she found it exciting and satisfying to have these new questions and perspectives to ponder. Her boss was super happy afterwards, and Margo even gave her a "great job" on the way out. Sara was sure that because of her new strategy about how she prepared, she did add more value than she usually did, and it certainly boosted her confidence. She felt less transactional and more strategic. She also jotted down some notes for next time.

Now that Sara's more aware of what her boss, other senior leaders, and even the board care about, she'll approach presentations from a different perspective. She is able to imagine the kinds of questions he's going to have to answer from his boss. She loves the simple question Melissa gave her: **What does someone 2 levels up care about?** This question just makes it so clear. If she can present to that – which she knows she can – this will make their jobs easier and give them the right insight which overall will make everyone happy.

After Sara filled Melissa in on all the details, Melissa jumped in and added, "You got it. And remember, you don't want to ask, **'What does someone two levels up from me care about?'** only when you have a presentation. This is a good question to stop and reflect on periodically (maybe even daily) just to get yourself into a higher level of thinking. I'm really happy for you, Sara. So now tell me, **"What would success look like at the end of our session today?"**

"I've been thinking about how important it is to spend time thinking intentionally," Sara answered. "I'm trying to put that into practice. I'm also working on being more intentional about what's on my to-do list everyday. And I'm noticing that I have some big items on my list that I need to plan out within the next year or so. I'm not great at prioritizing them because they're not urgent. There always seems to be something more pressing to do. Basically, I work on them when I find the time."

Melissa understood this common derailer all too well. At a certain level in an organization, manager, director and higher up, the responsibilities and must-do's become almost daunting. The list gets very long and people like Sara become very busy. But it always comes down to this: Are you doing the things you need to achieve your vision for success, or do you get so caught up with urgent requests or other people's priorities that your longer-term priorities, goals, and aspirations get lost?

Do you tend to think first about the issues or situations where you need to step in to help out? Or do your biggest priorities relate only to what's urgent or has pressing deadlines? It's not that these are wasted time or effort because they are useful to the organization, but it's not very intentional to only pay attention to what's urgent and you might not be spending time on what's most useful to the organization over the longer term. It's reacting to things rather than intentionally choosing them. Sara works in an organization as part of a team, and also cares a lot about helping people. It's normal and expected that she would spend some time on other people's priorities and on organizational priorities sometimes, and even on what's most pressing today. But each person is hired to add a specific value to the organization, and you can add a lot more value if you're really clear what your bigger priorities are, your strategic priorities, and where you're most expected to add value over the longer term. It's about really knowing what's most important for you to be working on – from a strategic perspective to provide the most value from someone at your level, not just solving problems, filling gaps, and reacting to deadlines. The word "important" is key to define here, because most of the leaders I know aren't wasting their time doing things that are *unimportant* for the organization – instead, they're usually derailed by spending too much time, effort, and energy on things that are important for the organization, but not the most important things for *them* to be working on to make progress on strategic and longer term goals.

Melissa acknowledged Sara, saying, "I get it. You want to help and you're also a 'doer,' so you just jump right in when you're needed."

Sara laughed. "You really know my derailers, don't you?"

"Trust me, Sara," Melissa said, "you're not alone! Automatically saying yes to people or stepping in to help is the way most of us roll. We love helping someone solve their problems or being part of their success in one way or another. And you're someone who thrives on it. I think that since you started coaching with me, this is something you're more aware of. Being intentional with what you choose to spend time on, and what you say yes to (either explicitly or implicitly) is one of the reasons we're here."

This is an important aspect of being strategic with regards to moving your priorities forward. Your priorities need the same space, time, and attention that you give to others. You can support others to move ahead with their priorities, but without doing the work for them or saving them with all the answers. That makes for a big win.

Melissa and Sara talked about being "reactive" instead of "intentional." Being reactive is doing something because of a request or a deadline or even an automatic response rather than intentionally deciding to spend time on something else, even if that something else might not be deemed urgent, or due right now or top of mind on anyone's radar. Oftentimes, leaders gravitate to what they're good at or what they're most comfortable doing, or of course what is most urgent or most "on fire." Getting away from this usual response, means developing a strategy for leaders to change their mindset.

Be conscious about what you say yes to. It's a funny word — "helping". Helping doesn't mean doing it for you. Maybe it's enabling someone else to do it. Maybe it's providing a high-level opinion about something. Maybe it's choosing to do something longer-term that keeps the business moving forward towards its strategic goals rather than getting caught up in the chaos of the moment.

Also, be conscious about what you might say "no" to. Or "not now," or "this is what I can do instead" like "I can provide the most value by talking to them for 10 minutes about this—instead of doing the work for them for four hours" or—even better try this more often -- "you can handle it." Ask yourself, **"A year from now, what's most important for me to pay attention to this week to get to the future I've envisioned?"** By changing your mindset, being less reactionary, paying attention to the right things, everyone benefits.

At this point in their session, Melissa decided it was the right time to talk about Stephen Covey's Big Rocks. The concept, popularized in the 1990s in his books, has been used and modified over the years, and many people use the term Big Rocks, and Covey's concept, in slightly different ways.

Think of your long list of to-dos as a bucket filled with sand, pebbles, and Big Rocks. We all have sand, pebbles, and Big Rocks in our jobs but it's how we fill our buckets that will determine what we get done.

Melissa uses 'Big Rocks' as a metaphor for longer-term, major strategic objectives—the ones that matter most in the areas you lead. They are the two or three bigger-picture goals you're primarily responsible for and can have a substantial impact on over a period of about a year.

You may also have short-term priorities that are urgent because of deadlines but those aren't the priorities we're talking about. There may also be other very important longer-term goals and initiatives that others are most responsible for and are very important to the organization, but you want to be very clear about what yours are.

Here's the secret: prioritize *your* three Big Rocks. While you'll always contribute to others' priorities, clarity about your own Big Rocks is crucial. For instance, Sara might have a Big Rock around ensuring their supply chain is as environmentally progressive and stable. That's the Big Rock. Sara might lead a series of initiatives that support that Big Rock like creating a Scorecard Dashboard for suppliers to track reductions in energy and water consumption or waste production amongst their suppliers, for example. These specific project initiatives support the Big Rock. She might have priorities within each project that support the Big Rock of moving the organization forward with respect to their supply chain vision.

Next in the bucket are the pebbles: the day-to-day tasks, projects, and efforts likely important to the organization, and possibly even Sara's role, but don't directly feed into or support her Big Rocks (for instance, she might be required to overhaul a specific process in one of her plants. It might be needed and expected, but it doesn't feed into her Big Rock. Or it might be that she's asked to help out on some important work for the organization that fits into someone else's Big Rock, so it might still be very important to the organization, but of lesser importance to her).

Lastly, there is a lot of sand that we all spend time on – these are tasks that need to get done but they don't directly help you progress on your Big Rocks. These might be something like filling out timesheets or approving expenses or creating a job posting for a new hire or something like that. They're still important to the organization (and they might feed into someone else's Big Rocks) and you will still handle these (or delegate them), but your primary focus should be on your Big Rocks. Presumably if the organization is asking you to do it, it has to be done for a reason—but if you fill your bucket first with sand and pebbles, there is no room for the Big Rocks.

This is exactly what happens with leaders' time. You need to focus on your Big Rocks first. When you get derailed by other people's priorities, or when you get stuck in the smaller details, your bigger projects suffer. I'll reiterate because I think it's important: a part that many people misunderstand or overlook is that sometimes your pebbles and sand might be someone else's Big Rocks. I think that's what really confuses people sometimes. In the case of the submitting expenses in a timely fashion, for instance, it might link to a Finance person's Big Rock around an initiative to streamline expenses that they have to present at a second quarter board meeting. So, it is important for you to complete them, even if it doesn't relate to your Big Rocks. You just want to be aware and intentional about how you're spending your time.

The key to figuring all of this out is really knowing your Big Rocks. And the reason I like using the term Big Rocks instead of 'priorities' is oftentimes the word priority ends up getting confused with what's on our to-do list and it's most often driven by a looming deadline or it's on fire or it's urgent in some way. But it might not be a Big Rock in the way we're using it here.

As Melissa described the Big Rocks concept, Sara's body practically shook with resonance.

"I can't tell you how much I get it. I spend a lot of time on things that are important to the company but are not really my priority—or my Big Rocks, if you will. In fact, I'm easily overwhelmed by this. There are even times that I catch myself feeling resentful. Getting involved in matters that don't really belong to me and don't move me forward. And trudging through my to-do list but not feeling like I make progress on the big things. I do it to myself, I know. But I honestly don't even know how to stop. My thinking is that if it's good for the company, shouldn't I be saying yes and getting involved? Meanwhile, there are strategic initiatives of my own that I'm not getting to. Again, because I'm so stretched that I don't always have enough time to work on them.

Melissa listened and then said, "I'll repeat what I've said before: Time management is simply about where you choose to spend your time. It's a simple concept, but not always easy to implement. Remember, **be intentional about what you're choosing**. Your Big Rocks help you stay on track with what's important, help you stay strategic, and help you make good choices with your time."

Next Melissa asked Sara, "Do you know what your two to three Big Rocks are? The ones you are most responsible for to forward in the next six to twelve months?"

Sara answered, "I do."

Even though oftentimes Big Rocks might be big concepts, or their delivery might seem far in the future, these Big Rocks need your time, energy, and attention. As a leader in any organization, the Big Rocks are things that you're most responsible for. Not the things that you're reacting to. So not all the emails, not urgent deadlines, not working on someone else's rocks. In my experience, most people are derailed by working on other people's Big Rocks without realizing that it's taking away from their own. Of course, there may be times that emails, deadlines, or someone else's requests relate to your Big Rocks too. And there are times— probably even daily—when you contribute to or help others with their Big Rocks. You are part of a team, part of an organization and you want to be a good colleague. Just be more *intentional* about your time, and about making sure you're moving forward your Big Rocks and being more intentional about *how* you help others whether that's your team, your peers, or the people senior to you.

Sara continued, "You got me thinking, Melissa. This conversation is taking me back to your favourite question about what success looks like to me. It doesn't look or feel like success to me when I say yes to everybody else and not to myself. And I know that when I'm thinking that I should be working on what I call 'my more important things,' at that moment, I'm not doing something right. The next time I catch myself there, I'm going to stop and ask, 'Sara, does prioritizing this feel like success to you? And am I being strategic?'"

Melissa gave her a big smile. Sara was really catching on to a new way of thinking that is strategic and forward moving. "That's it, Sara, you got it! Love it!"

Sara grew quiet. "Can I be candid with you about something?"

"Of course," Melissa replied. "All that happens here is just between us."

"Okay," Sara said, "So, this whole thing about not getting to my Big Rocks bothers me. A lot. For one thing, one of my rocks is a huge initiative that is very important to me. It fills me with purpose and creativity, and when I'm working on it, I feel myself come alive. It's a plant-wide process improvement that will reduce waste, energy, and water consumption. I'm about a year now into it and I'm so close to being ready to show what I've come up with. I just know they're going to be all over it when I get it together. And it's going to have a huge impact on the company. Lately, though, when I sit down to work on it, boom, I get called away.

"This is one thing that I dislike about working for a big organization. My priorities are not recognized as organizational priorities. On the one hand, there's a lot of opportunity for me to grow here and to make a difference, but, not to sound selfish or anything, I give so much to everyone and I know this comes with the territory but…well…if I'm to be honest about it, sometimes I feel sorry for myself."

> It's not always easy to prioritize your Big Rocks because let's face it, there's a lot of overlap in organizations. It might even be confusing because sometimes your Big Rock overlaps a Big Rock for someone else, but maybe you have slightly different priorities or responsibility areas, or you might be expected to add value in a different way around those Big Rocks.
>
> What can you do to prioritize your Big Rocks?
>
> First, start by knowing what your Big Rocks are. A big chunk of your time should go to your own Big Rocks. Get clear on what your responsibilities, functions, and tasks are within it. Pay attention to how much of your week you spend on the things you're responsible for to move forward.

When Melissa asks clients to stop and reflect on how much time they actually spend on their Big Rocks, many regretfully say they spend only about 25% of time or less on their own Big Rocks. While there's no magic number to aim for, and the ideal number varies significantly at different levels and in different roles, it's likely that it should be more than 50% and maybe even 60-70% of your time on your Big Rocks. These targets are made-up numbers, but whatever the magic number is for you, it probably should be higher than 20%. If you work in an organization, the number is almost never as high as 90% or 100% (unless you have a singular area of focus like a highly specialized expert working on one project or something like that). It's expected and gracious that you contribute to the organization in many ways. But this exercise is about awareness and intention, not a hard target. Take inventory: What are you giving your time to? Where is your time being spent unintentionally? What do you get called in to do that doesn't feel like one of your Big Rocks?

This doesn't mean don't spend time with or support peers or direct reports. In fact, that's an essential part of good leadership. It might even be one of your Big Rocks—in fact most senior leaders do have at least one Big Rock that relates to creating a diverse and inclusive culture, or developing talent to enable others to be the best they can be to leverage their strengths, and to help them feel engaged and supported. But enabling someone isn't the same as doing it for them. In a well-designed system, everyone's Big Rocks are well-defined and clear and cascade up to and down so that everyone's Big Rocks are interconnected and support organizational goals, and everyone supports each other intentionally, rather than haphazardly. When this is the case, it's much easier to hit those higher percentages of time mentioned above because if you focus on your Big Rocks, you actually help others succeed in theirs too.

"The aspect of bringing your awareness into what you're doing is the first piece of being able to move forward your Big Rocks," Melissa told Sara. "If you're not conscious of something, then you can't choose it. You're just in it.

"Another piece is knowing what your role is. Some rocks are not yours only. Some are so big that there are different parts to them and not all of it belongs to you. Sometimes, someone will pick such a Big Rock that we think everything related to it is ours but really our role is a specific thing and someone or someone else has a different role.

"It's true that it's not always clear. It could happen that sometimes you get caught up in other people's excitement. And then your mind starts going a mile a minute and the next thing you know you're having fun with their stuff instead of your own. This commonly happens in the workplace.

"And even though forwarding your Big Rocks might not be time sensitive, or be needed now or urgently, if you're almost never doing anything to forward them, where will you be in six or twelve months from now when your projected date to have accomplished this arrives?"

Sara nodded but added, "That all sounds great in theory, but even with clear Big Rocks, it still feels like I might have trouble distinguishing whether I should spend time on something or not. There are a lot of tasks that I'm not sure if they fall within my Big Rocks, or even if I'm sure they do, I'm not sure if I should be focusing on them at that moment."

"I can help you with this," Melissa reassured her. "Are you familiar with the urgent vs important matrix? Another tool in *The Seven Habits of Highly Effective People* that Stephen Covey popularized is the Eisenhower's Time Management Matrix. In it, he talks about managing what to focus on at any time.

"I'm not familiar with any of this," Sara admitted.

"This matrix helps people clarify their priorities and do something about them. It's the awareness piece of 'how am I doing with this? Am I doing enough to get to where this needs to be in six or twelve months or whatever it is?' It helps people think about what is future-oriented for themselves versus the present tasks, projects, and usual day to day stuff. It's not about perfection or not like a binary thing. It's a way to forward their own Big Rocks. It is a very reliable strategy that many people in leadership roles use to create momentum. It helps people see where time gets pulled away from them.

"So," Sara wondered out loud, "I should be asking myself the question, 'Am I using my time wisely here?' Especially when I'm with my direct reports because, as I've already established, in my mind I believe I must be available to their every beck and call. This is also true with how I am with my bosses and my peers, too."

"Yes," Melissa added. "And it's not that you must say no to people and things that pull time away from you. You *might* say no. Or it might be that you say yes differently. The same goes for time spent with peers and higher ups. Remember you told me that you sometimes feel overwhelmed and resentful? That's a good place to start poking around. Pull your awareness into those situations that make you feel you're not in the right place."

"Yeah," Sara said as she slowly exhaled. "That makes sense."

The awareness of how you're spending your time is the first step towards helping you shift the bar and intentionally start moving out of those situations that unnecessarily pull your time away from forwarding your Big Rocks. The matrix helps you look at your time a little differently than the Big Rocks, although they're absolutely related and using the concepts together will be even better.

The "urgent versus important" matrix helps organize your workload and priorities. It's a classic tool that a lot of high achieving people use to help them use their time well and I'm confident this matrix will help you, too. This

	Urgent	Not Urgent
(Your) Important	Your **Important** Work (aligns with your Big Rocks) + **Urgent**	Your **Important** Work (aligns with your Big Rocks) + **Not Urgent**
Not (Your) Important	Work **Not Important** to you (might be to someone else) + **Urgent**	Work **Not Important** to you (might be to someone else) + **Not Urgent**

matrix can help you visually to catch when you're doing such things, unintentionally being distracted.

Most people spend their time in quadrants urgent/ important and urgent/not important boxes, the two urgent boxes. But again, the word "important" here is a bit tricky. A lot of people think that as long as they're doing something important for the organization, they're doing great, and this is not completely true. In my experience, most leaders aren't spending their time on unimportant things. But if we want to use this matrix to help us manage our time, we have to recognize that 'unimportant' means 'unimportant' to *their* Big Rocks. Or maybe their role within those Big Rocks. It might be important to the organization, but not "*your* something important." It might be someone else's Big Rock. You can add some value at times, but it's not in your important quadrant.

Your 'important' will definitely include tasks related to forwarding your Big Rocks but will also likely be a bit broader than that too. Also, in some cases, the word "important" can be replaced by the word "strategic." From a strategic point of view, you might want to be a little ruthless about what is in your important category. Think about your role in it. For the purposes of time management anyway. You might not have to be as ruthless in your interactions—it's just a way to reflect and choose consciously.

Now, look at quadrant two, the important/not urgent box. This is where you want to spend the bulk of your time. Because ideally you're working on things that are important before they become urgent.

Sara had an admission. "When I see things in front of me with closer deadlines, that's the work I gravitate towards. I almost always end up choosing the most immediate... just like – it's the next thing that we're looking to complete, so why not just do it and get it out of the way? Do you know what I mean?"

"Well, that's true for most of us, and it also might continue to be true for you at least for a bit until you develop new habits," Melissa answered. "You might have to spend some of the time in the urgent / important quadrant, especially at first, but ideally we want to shift away from the urgent as much as possible. But here's the amazing part: if you start to shift your time to the important/non-urgent quadrant and implement some of the other techniques we've talked about like booking time in your calendar and such, there will be a lot less showing up in the urgent quadrants because you will be on top of those strategic and important things earlier.

Sara then asked Melissa to explain how she could link this matrix tool with her Big Rocks.

"With regards to the matrix, here's what I do with mine," Melissa answered. "I take my to-do list and I just plot it on the four squares of a graph that I create. I might even label the ones that are my Big Rocks and I look at where my time is going and how my current to-do list corresponds with my Big Rocks, and where I need to spend time strategically. It's like I use a few different tools to see the bigger picture: the Big Rocks, the to-do list which tends to be a bit more heavily weighted on immediate tasks and deadlines, any timelines or milestones that I need to track to, my Strategic To-Do List and the urgent-versus-important matrix.

"Of course, it's not easy to switch from urgent to non-urgent right away but seeing it in front of me helps me think about where I want to focus my time. Where we want to be is in the important/non-urgent square as much as possible and so, when I see that I'm not, I adjust.

"In reality, this should all only take a couple minutes. It's just a quick way to give you a meta-view of where you're spending your time and where you should be spending your time. This matrix is a quick visual way for people, especially those pulled in every direction and with great demands on their time and energy to plot time and see where it's going.

"Remember, we're not likely to hit 100% of our time on our Big Rocks. We're just trying to raise you from 20% to maybe something closer to 60-70%, depending on your role.

Even though you think you know where your time is going, it'll surprise you what's revealed when you track it. And, if you find something that shows up continuously in the non-urgent not-important box, you might ask, why is it even on your list? If you decide it shouldn't be, and then you remove it, it frees up mental space and energy. It's very liberating."

Sara said this out loud to imprint it into her psyche. "I should be doing strategic and important things, especially those that contribute directly to moving my Big Rocks, before they become urgent."

"Yes," Melissa added, "I want you to get better at choosing what you spend time on and when. This strategy will help you with forwarding your rocks and will also alleviate a lot of the overwhelm. The best part? It takes almost no time at all to do this exercise. The busier you are, the more likely you should plot this out. I often hear leaders saying they just need to "free up time." That is extremely difficult. It's very rare that people free up enough time to make any kind of difference in their strategic or important goals. Honestly, you just have to *choose* where you spend your time. And, if you are regularly asking yourself the question, 'what does success look like for me in six months or a year from now' this tool can serve you well to bring that vision of success closer.

"We're almost at time, so you know I'm going to ask: **"What will you commit to before our next session?"**

"Well, that's an easy one," Sara answered quickly. "To clearly identify my two or three Big Rocks and my ideal role within them. I'll define what success would look like a year from now for each of these Big Rocks. And I'll use the urgent versus important matrix at least a few times before we meet next—more if it's needed."

Sara couldn't wait to start using this strategy. In fact, she was even thinking of making it a competition. Between her and herself. How much could she move from driven by urgent things to more intentional, longer-term and strategic activities? Sara wanted people to notice and hear them say, 'Sara had a great year!' That's part of her success vision: Recognition!

CHAPTER 9

What Do You Want to Create Versus What Do You Want to Fix?

*"The measure of a society is not only
what it does but the quality of its aspirations."*
— *Wade Davis*

Sara was not looking forward to meeting with Melissa today. She was feeling like she had let herself down between the last session and this one and so came into this session with a general feeling of depletion.

To start the session, Melissa jumped right in with her classic question, which only served to trigger Sara even more. "It's good to see you again, Sara! So tell me, **what successes have you had since the last session?**

Sara answered with a don't-get-me-started tone in her voice. "Hmph, I don't know about successes. I don't feel like I had any. What keeps popping up for me is the same struggle I always have; I am easily overwhelmed, and I want to know how to handle the overwhelm when the daily tasks start to pile up. I almost always immediately end up pulling myself away from the creative thinking that I love doing or from the Big Rock stuff and start handling the more pressing matters."

Melissa empathized with her. "I hear you. This is a real problem for most people. Everyone's days are packed with meetings and phone calls, team members needing help or wanting to pick their brains, requests from others, deadlines— lots of things pulling you in many directions. It's what keeps us in reactive mode rather than intentional mode. We're reacting to and responding to other priorities and it's hard to be intentional about our own Big Rocks, and most important focus areas."

The requests, the day-to-day work, the urgent deadlines, problems that need attention—these never really go away. And sometimes it can even make the strategic work, the Big Rocks, the most important areas to focus on feel like a terrible distraction. This is where, especially in those moments when people feel overwhelmed that they need to think about what success looks like to them. This is where bringing awareness to your vision, purpose, and planning is very important to get you to where you want to be. Hold a snapshot in your mind of you there already: **What would success look like in that ideal end-state?** Really connect with that desired future emotionally too. **What would you feel? What would you notice?** And then think about the three most important things to pay attention to, to get closer to that end-state, that desired future. Something you have to *choose* to spend time on. Even when you don't feel like you have the time. Because no matter how much time you spend on the other requests and to-dos that pop up, your list will *always* be unfinished. You might as well intentionally choose some time for the important stuff too because reacting is not a strategy.

Even though Sara *knows* this, in her heart of hearts, her default is still to drop everything for a pressing deadline and for other people vs. what's fundamentally important.

Sara said, "I hear you and I know it's really a question of me getting myself to do more of what I need to do for me. I guess if I think about it, maybe there has been a shift in the past few weeks since we last met, actually. I have been delegating more and letting go of controlling the outcome. I'm also getting better at putting some self-imposed deadlines on the things that help me with my Big Rocks."

"See," Melissa said, "you *did* have some successes since last time!"

"Ha-ha, I guess you're right." Sara thought about it more. "I had sort of forgotten I've been better at this. I usually start with asking myself the question I know you love so much: **What would success look like in six months**? And then I choose a few things to focus on. So, I guess I did make some progress in this area, after all. I still have a long way to go, though."

Melissa asked, "**What have you noticed when you've been able to stay focused on your most important and strategic work?**"

One thing that Sara noticed immediately was that when she brought attention to where she wanted to go—on her Big Rocks and her more strategic priorities—she was able to shift out of being reactive and she felt less frantic. She got more of her own work done. And when she felt less pulled in all directions, she was able to pay attention to how she could add value rather than automatically diving into the work itself. This helped her to help others in a more meaningful way. She felt more settled and was able to make a little more progress on the important, less urgent things. It actually felt much better than she had expected. And she didn't feel the burden of thinking, *Now I have more work to do.* Taking a little more time with people for a quick conversation about whatever the issue is keeps the task on their list where it belongs, instead of it being added to her to-do list. When Sara thought it through, she realized there have been some successes — she just wasn't noticing them.

Melissa was delighted when Sara shared this. "Exactly what we want to see! Small shifts in intentionality and behaviour make a big difference in impact—on yourself, on others and on the work!

"When you're feeling overwhelmed, the solution is not to keep doing more urgent things, but really choosing: **What's the big picture here? What are my Big Rocks? What are the most important things for me to focus on that will move my Big Rocks, leverage my value, and achieve my priorities rather than someone else's?** As I said before, there is nothing wrong with helping others with their priorities: we just want to do it intentionally.

Melissa continued, "You know I'm also going to ask: **What would success look like for you at the end of our session today?"**

"Well," Sara answered, "I wanted to talk about planning for the future. As an organization we're starting to do some strategic planning for the next five to seven years, and it just feels so far away. I find it so hard to know how to contribute. I'm concerned because I haven't had time to read the industry publications to know what the trends are. I don't even know where to find the time to catch up. How will I predict the operational changes that are needed or what trends are affecting us if I'm not caught up? To use your language, success would be that I have a better sense of what I'm doing with respect to the strategic planning—that I'm ready and intentional and also that I add value at a strategic level in all of these meetings."

Melissa nodded. "So far, we've talked a lot about being more strategic in the moment and on a day-to-day basis. And I am glad we spent time on that because it's the most overlooked part of being strategic. But we should also talk about what most people think about when they hear they need to be more strategic and that is the more formal and structured part of being strategic: strategic planning, budget planning, resource planning. It is very important in organizations. The structure, cycle, and outputs of these are there to make sure we actually do the reflection and thinking for the coming year, since we usually have deadlines and meetings and requirements related to them. It makes sure we're intentional about where we're heading as an organization.

"Some of this planning is related to looking back (what happened in the past year or two, what themes or trends are we noticing about what happened, why did things occur the way they did, what worked well, what could have worked better, etc.).

"Some of the planning is related to looking outside your sector. It's not important to get caught up in trends, but it is prudent to recognize and anticipate what the trends inside and outside of your sector are. For example, what is shifting in buying power, delivery, payment methods, and technology. You don't have to be the first to act, but there are some trends that if you don't adopt them, you might then find yourself reacting and this could mean you're late or maybe even too late. That said, attend certain seminars, read articles and/or follow your favourite thought leaders and consultants on social media. Or my personal favourite: ask a few other colleagues and experts what they're noticing—you'll get a very good indication of what's happening. You can bring what you're finding to the table internally and brainstorm to understand what a trend's implications might be. This will allow your longer-term decision making to reflect possible changes inside and outside your sector.

"And, of course, some parts of strategic planning are related to looking forward. The forward-looking part is often what makes people think they're not good at strategic planning. There is a lot of pressure to feel like you have to *predict* the future, which of course is very hard. In fact, most predictions about anything are notoriously wrong. But there's still value in going through these exercises.

"Let's also expand your understanding of what it means to be forward thinking. We talk about forecasting, modelling, and predictions, of course, which can be high-level or very detailed and sometimes complex. We most often look at these related to budgets, but we can also look at resources (predicting what resources we need in different areas of the business in the next year for instance), or related to how certain products might do, or related to market conditions, or operational efficiencies that might be required, etc. For more complex and high-cost decisions, we might also look at scenario planning which makes various assumptions of the future and how modifying those assumptions or other variables might influence the different outcomes of those scenarios. This can sometimes be quite extensive with complex models and calculations and such. For instance, if you're investing in a multi-million dollar facility that will last 20-30 years or longer, you might create different models based on different assumptions related to interest rates, energy prices, consumer behaviour, materials costs, delivery trends, technology evolution, and many other factors to get a range of potential scenarios that might play out depending on how different unknown variables *might* actually happen (but which we really can't predict). This helps give potential outcomes which in turn allows us to make better decisions, and consider various risks, even if we can't actually predict the future.

"All the things we've talked about so far (forecasting, predictions, scenario planning, etc.) -- these are all very *predictive* in nature—they rely on us trying to predict what might happen. But there are other approaches we can and should take when we're looking to the future and planning for it. Things that aren't necessarily predictive. One approach that I call the Imagine Exercise is more based on what is desired rather than simply predicted. You don't have to *know* what is going to happen, you just have to *want* for something better, *imagine* something better. These approaches that aren't 'predictive' are just as important to incite new ideas and inform future decisions."

Sara interjected at this point to say, "I'm intrigued."

Melissa added, "What I'm asking is that you imagine the year ahead in your mind in terms of what you *want* the year to look like, assuming everything played out in the best way possible. **What future would you create, what would success look like, and what would the after-picture look like in the best-case scenario?**"

Sara questioned her. "Um . . . so what are you saying? You want me to daydream?"

"Not exactly." Melissa answered. "Let's call it strategic imagination. Thinking about what you want the future to look like—with big, bold dreams and lofty goals; thinking big about what's possible, even if it seems unattainable."

Apple's Steve Jobs embodied this approach. He refused to limit his thinking or be limited by other people's thinking either. He didn't care about being practical or predictive while he was imagining the future in technology. He came up with stuff that the rest of the world thought impossible, or perhaps that the technology didn't exist yet. For him, there was no taking "no." His approach: imagine the idea and then figure out how to make it happen.

Patagonia is another great example. They have always had enviable environmental and social responsibility programs that are at the heart of everything they do. They dreamed consciousness into the very fabric of their operations, and they found the 'how' to make it their business practice. They build on what they've already done, they are very clear about what they stand for. It's all part of their vision. To the point where if it doesn't align with their values, they don't do it. And this is even posted on their website; "we use our resources; business, investment, voice and imagination—to do something about countering the threat of extinction." This is bold for an organization. They consider 'our voice' and 'our imagination' as resources. And if you watch them in action, so much of what they do as a company actually aligns with this. They're not just words on a website.

And while they've always been a leader in this, in 2022, in planning his succession, Patagonia founder, 83-year-old Yvon Chouinard made the unprecedented decision to give it all away. He gave this three-billion dollar company that nets 100 million profit a year to a trust that will use its profits to fight climate change. This just goes to show that what can be imagined, can be done.

Patagonia is only one of so many examples. This kind of big picture, future thinking is not exclusive to the people at Patagonia.

Sara says, "Well, those examples are amazing, and certainly inspiring, but I'm not Steve Jobs or Yves Chouinard."

Melissa said, "And you don't have to be. Every leader who wants to grow personally and professionally needs to grow their ability to imagine and to future-think. You can do this in your own way, in your own areas. You can do this on your own, with your team, with your peers in the executive team, or with your superiors."

"Let's say we're talking about the team you manage. You can lead some exercises to co-create with your team, get excited about a big bold vision for what's possible. And remember, this isn't about being predictive, or even being bound by what's realistic, but imagining a better future, your loftiest aspirations. In fact, being predictive or being too realistic in this particular exercise limits your ability to picture new possibilities. We also don't look at *how* we could achieve this when we're doing this exercise—not yet at least. We bring in *how* and realism later. If we do it too soon, it doesn't allow for us to think big or to be creative or innovative about new possibilities. For now, we imagine."

Melissa is suggesting that Sara imagines something new and then plan for it. That seems doable, and even fun. She's encouraging Sara to be mindful about involving her team in creative thinking and to be strategic with it so it becomes something they can plan for.

Sara reflected, "No one here ever, at least not in my memory or in any direct way, has asked me to imagine and create and yet, ever since we started coaching together, one key message I'm taking away is to get my head out of the day-to-day grind sometimes to think more. And maybe imagine more. That's really exciting, actually. If I'm not caught up in predicting, or in trying to figure out how this could work or being limited by the resources I have or the budget, or the time, or what we've done already, I can totally see how that would allow my creative side to dream bigger, imagine bigger, especially for the passion areas I've described before. I feel like a big weight has just lifted off of me, which is surprising and exciting at the same time."

Sara shared an experience from last weekend when she was apple-picking with her kids. "It was a breezy, slightly cool gorgeous day with all the leaves changing. The kids ran around making up stories and I remember thinking just how open and free their little minds are. And oh, the things they say! And what a shame it is that we lose that sense of wonder."

"Here's an opportunity for you to call that sense of wonder back in and have some fun." Melissa continued. "For every leader wanting to incorporate new strategies for success, future thinking is a big piece of it. Imagining: this is the part where you are being creative and not afraid to dream up big bold ideas that can inspire change, sometimes even great change. This is an important piece of moving forward—both professionally and organizationally."

Sara countered, "But when I think about this year's budget planning and my Big Rocks and looking ahead six to twelve months, I'm still stuck on the details. And now I feel myself being drawn back to 'how' will we do whatever I'm imagining. It's like I imagine too big. And my team will resist this a bit. They're quite practical. So how would I lead an Imagine exercise like this?"

"Well, for a budgeting exercise for the next six to twelve months, there's probably a lot more practical involved than imagining," Melissa answered. "The timeline is short, and it's being used for planning purposes, and you need to have specifics rooted in reality for that particular exercise. It's not to say you could *never* use it for a budgeting exercise, but this might be more relevant to explore for something like: **what kind of organization you want to be three to five years from now**, or **what kind of products you would love to see your organization provide that would be amazing**, or **what kind of workplace culture you really want to see**, or even **what is possible in the growth for a person on your team**, imagining first without constraints is a great way to start.

"There are several ways to start, but in general, you'd want to set the context that this is a brainstorming session and that for the next hour, or whatever time you've chosen, you're going to imagine the best possible future for the organization, or for your team, or for your product, or maybe even for a particular initiative—whatever you're paying attention to. Make sure they know you will have another session on *how* you'll achieve it later, or maybe dedicate the last half an hour on *how* because some people will stress about it if you don't tell them you're going to get to that. Tell them that you promise you we will look at the practical pieces of it and how you're going to get there, just not yet. For now, forget what is practical or feasible.

"During this Imagine time, make some agreements that anything goes, no judgment, no pointing out (yet) why something won't work or what the risks are, no focusing on how to get it done. They just have to imagine a better future without worrying about problems, risks, cost, other restrictions, etc.

Prompt them with questions like:

- **What would we want this to look like if we weren't bound by cost, time, resources, etc.?**
- **One year from now, in the best-case scenario, what would success look like?**
- **What would we want our customers to be saying about us two years from now?**
- **What would they be saying about our products?**
- **What kind of market share would we have?**
- **What would we be known for in the industry?**

"Of course, every leader can reframe the questions they pose to their particular scenario. And questions that will nudge your team to think bigger and be bolder about the future. Maybe they say: we want to be the number one supplier of packaging made completely of food scraps compostable materials. Be as bold as you can be.

"Another tactic is to focus on what you want rather than what you don't want. Just like you're supposed to tell a kid who is running at the pool "Walk" instead of "Don't run" if you don't want them to slip on the wet concrete. Name what you want. Here you want them to paint the best possible version of what's possible. Nudge them to think bigger. Or if they start with something they don't want, that's okay, just follow it up by asking: "that's great—**so if that's something you don't want, what would you want instead?**" They might need a bit of help reframing so if you're the one leading this initiative, you could also say: If you don't want our customers to think our product is difficult to use, it sounds like you want it to be easy to use by someone who doesn't have training in it" or whatever it might be. And they might adjust what you said, but it gives them a starting point."

"Hmmm," Sara interjected, "I would love to impose some rules before we start."

Melissa suggested, "What about co-creating some agreements? If you co-create them, they'll be more likely to follow them. But, of course, you get to put your wishes on the table too.

"Some agreements that you might want them to commit to could be simply to let them know and ask them to agree that no idea is too crazy or too out-there not to be put on the whiteboard for consideration. And that everyone supports and encourages everyone else in their creative thinking. And that every contribution made is without judgement.

"Now, imagine this playing out. Probably the best ideas will receive the most noise and excitement and that can be fun for your group—and you—to witness. Granted, some people in the group will be too uncomfortable at first to contribute but if this Imagine exercise is done pretty regularly, you'll find over time that more and more people will relax, let go and have fun with it.

"Most people in leadership positions probably already know who the most creative and innovative thinkers are and who their most practical step-by-step doers are and when you put them all in a room together to go through this process it becomes infectious. The practical doers will hear a far-out idea that they love and their wheels will start to turn. "How can we do this and what steps will we need to take to get there?" It's actually okay if certain people contribute more strongly in this Imagine stage, and the practical people shine when we turn it into action.

Strategic leadership is bold vision PLUS action

"We need both. We just start with the bold vision first because if we start with the actions or the practical or the "how" first, the ideas may not be as bold as they could be.

Melissa continued reassuring Sara that in her 25+ years of coaching leadership strategy to Directors and C-suite executives, she saw over and over again how impactful this type of strategic brainstorming is. Dreamers get to dream, doers get to do and everyone, each with their own strengths, gets to interact in the creation of something new. It wouldn't work with only one or the other. Everyone needs to be willing to throw caution to the wind and when they do, magic happens.

This exercise idea was catching on for Sara. "I am definitely excited about this and committed to doing it. And I can see how this could help our brainstorming become bolder with what's possible. But there is a small part of me that is still hesitant to bring forward some of my bolder concepts that I've been thinking about. The ideas really push the boundaries of our current trajectory as a company at the intersection of sustainability, consumerism, social justice, and systemic change, but I think the timing might be premature. I'm not sure we'd be ready to implement any of this in the near future."

Melissa encouraged Sara to articulate the vision she has and decide when and where to share that vision.

"Amanda Gorman, the young inaugural poet, was daring us to dream about some pretty big ideas. But she didn't wait until we were ready to hear them (in fact, that's often when these visions are most needed). And to build on what we were saying earlier: she didn't list off statistics and try to predict the future or try to stay within the bounds of what might be deemed to be 'realistic'. Instead, she captured our hearts, challenged our thinking and beliefs around societal norms, and inspired us to continue to value and fight for social justice. And she didn't wait until we were ready to hear them, until the conditions were right. In fact, most often, that's exactly when we need to hear them the most."

Sara frowned. "Well, as iconic as her speech was, it doesn't seem like anything is being achieved by it."

Melissa gave more context. Sometimes a vision is about igniting a spark in others to dare to hope for a better future, to inspire them when it feels hard, when the work is frustrating and complex. The more complex and systemic the change is, the more we sometimes need to tap into reasons to keep going. And a compelling vision does that. When you're looking to make multi-faceted, societal, and widespread behavioural and system change, you need a fearless vision. There is value in the dream itself. That's the important message. It gives you and others something to aspire to, something to aim for, a bolder direction than if you had a smaller goal that felt more achievable at that time. Imagining and dreaming a better future is so often overlooked since it gets discounted as not realistic especially in a certain timeline or with certain parameters.

And in an organization, you're usually focused on something smaller than some of the societal systemic change mentioned above—maybe being the number one choice for a certain product, or changing processes or materials to be more sustainable. In an organization, we're trying to get everyone actively working towards the same vision. And also, once you imagine a vision in an organization, the next step is to translate this into an actual plan with milestones and actions and accountability—all the structure to help it move forward and gain momentum. That all being said, in an Imagine exercise I'd really encourage you to think big and bold–much bigger and bolder than you would normally would. Most visioning in an organization plays too small and too safe. Tap into deep hunger and longing for what could be. At this stage, there are no limits to what is possible except for the limits you put on yourselves.

In a company, the vision is a starting point, but then you take what you imagined, and turn it into something to make it real. But you have to start with an exciting and compelling and even bold desired future.

"I see what you mean," Sara said. "If I'm thinking about my Big Rocks and this budget planning coming up, there are potential futures that can play out. But what I'm hearing is that I should do some of the predictive stuff, but also pay attention to what we *want* to happen what we truly desire, build some alignment around that, and then make plan actions with milestones and accountability to make it happen. Maybe even put some timelines, say three years from now, what do we want this to look like and in twelve months from now, what will it look like? And so on. Dream big, throw all the ideas out there and then decide on what the best vision of the future is, and then work backwards. Give it a framework with a roadmap and action plan to work on it over time. Yes?"

"Exactly," Melissa agreed.

To clarify her understanding of this Imagine exercise and the benefits that come from getting creative together as a team, she shared with Melissa this analogy of her kitchen redesign.

Ever since Sara and her partner bought their house, they'd been dreaming of updating the kitchen. They had been imagining the renovation since 2014—they created vision boards, cut out pictures from magazines, bookmarked websites with some of their Imagine photos. They made note of tile designs and colors, the accessories like chairs and countertop options. And they imagined what it would feel like to sit in those specific chairs at the island with the paint colors. They know what they want and even made a note of the stores to shop at.

Sara told Melissa that they were constantly adding ideas to the folders with all the things they love and want. And she assured Melissa that there was no question that as soon as they have enough set aside for it, they're doing it. They put a predetermined amount of money into a kitchen reno account.

Sara finished her story. "We're at the stage where we're ready to start planning our design. Financially, we're almost there. In our minds we already have our dream kitchen and now we need to take the practical steps to make it happen."

"I can hear the excitement in your voice, see your face light up when you talk about it," Melissa said. "That's what a good vision is—it should almost make you salivate, you want it so badly. Basically, yeah, you were dreaming about what you want your kitchen to be. You started with the big and bold Imagine piece."

"You know what, Melissa?" Sara said, "I want to thank you. Our sessions together are really convincing me how important it is to spend time thinking. I knew this before, but I didn't really take it as seriously as I probably should have. Take this session for example. Having worked with you on becoming more strategic,

I understand that part of strategic leadership is thinking outside of the box. You're always reminding me not to dismiss big ideas when they come and that's been a problem for me—I don't let myself think big."

To all you leaders, maybe now is the time you stop labeling your ideas as too far out or too crazy and instead, start testing them. No matter what you do or where you work or what makes your heart sing and no matter what success looks like to you, when big ideas come to you, stay with them. Imagine them becoming real. New ideas change the way your department works, the way your organization functions and maybe even push the whole industry into a next best thing. Why not you?

Just think about what you want. Organizations need strategic thinkers who aren't afraid of putting their creativity to work. It can be big and aspirational, but it doesn't have to be. It can be something that fits wherever your passion lies, or it can be something like what you want the culture of the organization to be or something smaller like what outcomes you want from the end of a three-day retreat.

Your voice and your imagination are assets too. To choose what the future can be and to think boldly about it, to push way beyond the practical and the predictive. It's like, 'if I could choose the future what would I create?'

Sara continued, "I can see how this will help a bit for some of our longer-term strategic discussions, but if I were to take this and apply it to my approach to operational planning, or next year's strategic plan, or even the upcoming budget what else should I consider? This is all starting to feel a bit complex and maybe a bit nebulous."

Melissa nodded. "These are great questions. So to bring this all full circle to where we started our session today, formal strategic planning in organizations has many pieces but the most important benefit of the whole exercise taking the time to think and reflect whether that's an Imagine exercise, or some of the more practical, evaluative, or predictive exercises like forecasting, scenario planning, and many others. We then turn all of that into some kind of actionable plan. So next time we'll focus on using formalized frameworks to turn imagined ideas into reality.

"So let's recap for today," Melissa asked. "**What are your takeaways?**"

"When I prepare for strategic planning," Sara said with conviction, "I'll do a bit of predictive work (what trends do we know are coming that might affect the business, what are we hearing from our customers about how their wants are changing, etc.) Then maybe I'll look at the different scenarios to see how they might play out. I'll also spend some time using the Imagine approach (envisioning a bold version of the best future we would want to play out or create—in one year or two years or five years or whatever timeframe we choose)."

"Sounds good," Melissa said, then asked another question. **"What specifically will you commit to?"**

"Let's see…" Sara paused and thought for a moment. "There are a few things I'm going to do for sure. I'll put aside some imagine/envisioning time for myself and let my creativity and boldest ideas of the future come out. I'll also set up a couple strategic planning sessions with my peers and suggest we have one of those (or the beginning of one of those) with some of these Imagine questions. And I want to set one up with my team as well. Maybe you and I can design these a bit more specifically as we lead up to them. I also want to spend a bit of time thinking about trends and customer feedback and what I'm seeing in the industry. The excuse that I don't have time doesn't seem to cut it for me now. I know this is more important than a lot of what I spend my time on."

Sara was impressed with herself. "Wow," she said, "I'm not even feeling agitated by everything I just committed to. I can honestly say that since we've had these several coaching sessions, and the work I've done in between I feel like space is opening up for me. Like, as I reorganize my thoughts and restructure how I spend my time, I'm already feeling more successful. Right now, it might all be in my mind, but it feels very liberating."

Sara also added that for her, one of the biggest shifts is to not feel paralyzed when she can't predict the future. There's a lot of freedom in being able to imagine a better future, a better end-state. She knows it'll take more thinking time but instead of feeling like it's an additional thing to do she's actually excited about adding this creative aspect to the mix, so she and her team come together with a plan to make it real, all with the same direction and vision.

CHAPTER 10

Strategic Leadership Is Vision Plus Purpose Plus Action

"Vision without action is just a dream, action without vision just passes the time, and vision with action can change the world."
— *Nelson Mandela*

Melissa greeted Sara, then said, "Preparing for this session, I was reflecting on the wins and successes that you've had that I know about, and I just want to remark how just five or six months ago, by your own words, you were a busy leader who was bogged down in the day-to-day minutiae and I don't see that anymore. You totally took to what was offered and adapted yourself easily and quickly to implement the strategies."

Sara replied, "Thank you, yes, I'm feeling really good about myself these days. And I'm pretty excited about everything we talked about last time. I've booked an Imagine session with my team and another one with my peers for some bigger conversations around where we really want to make a difference on the sustainability side and also for some specific initiatives and products we've talked about here and there," Sara shared. "But I can use your help with how to integrate these into the formal strategic planning process. I also have a few additional questions about how to stay focused on the future when there are so many problems that pop up that need solving every day."

"Of course," Melissa assured her. "Let's start with integrating all of this with your formal strategic planning efforts in the organization. One thing that really helps is using some planning structures for your initiatives.

> There are likely formal templates and structures that your organization already uses, and you should use those to create formal documents to put everything into writing. In general, a formalized plan will have the bold vision statement, have a clear purpose, set goals and targets, and an action plan all of which many include strategic plans, roadmaps, three-year vision, one-year vision, milestones, metrics, specific projects or initiatives, accountability, etc. So, let's say, right now you and your team held a planning session and have a bold vision for an initiative. You look at what that is and why. You describe a collective purpose that you then complement with a formalized plan. And all these formal structures and documents have a cyclic element to them (i.e., some are completed every April or December or whenever the organization dictates) and that brings some structure to them as well.

> There's another simple structure that I really like to organize my thoughts or communication—not just for strategic planning but for anything. I call it my **What-Why-How**. These aren't the questions what/why/how, but more the structure.

- The **What** is the end-state or vision or ideal future—it's the direction we're headed and where we want to end up.
- The **Why** is the purpose or the benefits or the impact we want.
- The **How** is the approach, methodology, tasks, execution.

What and **Why** come first and as much as possible, get some alignment on these two so we're all headed in the same direction. **How** is where execution and to-do lists and selected approaches come in. The Imagine exercise we discussed last time, spends a lot of time reflecting on and answering **What** and **Why** questions. All those people that might not have liked the Imagine exercise, will be happier once you bring this **How** piece in. Keep breaking it down into milestones and create markers that go into making it happen. There's a lot of value in writing it out.

The **What** and **Why** actually enable **How** even more since the execution is now in a direction to achieve something more clearly defined and something people are excited about.

It was the same with the idea to put a man on the moon by the end of the decade: when John F. Kennedy made that statement in 1961, they didn't actually have the technology to put a man on the moon. But a bold and maybe even unrealistic vision was made, people working on it had a shared sense of vision and purpose (there are many books written about how this was strongly present throughout NASA at all levels) and those good at execution made it happen—history was made. There was commitment to make it happen once the spark of desire was ignited. Those working on it had a bold vision to work towards and were unified with their collective purpose. They came together in each of their areas of expertise to make it happen.

What-Why-How works for all kinds of situations, not just large strategic planning initiatives. People even use it in simple ways like when defining the ideal outcome or end-state of a meeting (i.e. **What**), **Why** they're having the meeting, and then they get into the details of **How** they're executing something. It works very well with strategic thinking, but it works really for anything. In fact, using this structure, actually *makes* the exchange even more strategic because it starts people off with the high level and big picture (**What** and **Why**) and then addresses the more tactical (**How**)."

"Hold on," Sara interrupted. "This **What-Why-How** works in all kinds of communication, right? Not just in formalized structures."

"That's right," Melissa affirmed. "In keeping with this train of thought, let's move on. You also want to have plans that link up and across and down the organization, that's to say, everything you set for any initiative or project needs to be in alignment with organizational goals, mission, and values; they should all cascade up into the organization's known goals over a long period of time. They also need to be aligned with departmental goals, missions, and values and trickle down to individual goals, team goals. And then individual team members should have goals and things like that relate to the action plans and the strategies and things. So, what you plan is cascading up and down. And ideally, this is also integrating into other goals across the organization."

Sara, taking it all in, said, "So what you're saying is that we provide a formalized structure within which we support what we're planning to be in alignment with the organization's known goals and we do this by naming it, naming what the end state is, to evaluate what success would look like, in a year, a few years and so on."

"Yes," Melissa answered. "It should align up, across, and down. And you also want to make sure you have identified some purpose about why you're doing this, what you hope to achieve, the purpose for it, how it fits into the organizational goals and purpose and to name the impact and benefits."

For the sake of clarification, Sara said out loud, "The concept of putting it all into a formalized plan and document then, is to have everything thought through and put in one place where all the concepts are added together, right? This way there are no gaps or oversights and whatever questions come up, the answers are in there."

"Yes," Melissa agreed. "If we were to boil it down to something you can digest and commit to memory, yes. Understanding the importance of having a formalized statement and plan makes real the formula of what strategic leadership is really all about. If I were to create a single statement to define strategic leadership, it would be:

Vision plus Purpose plus Action equals Strategic Leadership

"And if there was a way to make sure that your vision, purpose, and actions unfold it's in the formalized statement."

Sara noticed something odd about this. "I notice you don't use the word *goal* in this formula—what about goals? We all have them, and we all have to take actions to reach them, so I wonder why are we not talking about them?"

Well," Melissa explained, "Vision is really the aspiration of what success would actually look like in the best-case scenario if everything were to go as planned—what would we see, how would people behave, what experiences will we have, etc. The vision is what we long for, what we want for a better future, not necessarily something we know exactly how to achieve yet. The energy of a goal is a bit more outcome-based, more achievement based. That's the difference."

There are different ways to use the word 'vision'. Many people use 'vision' as something grand about a whole team or whole department or whole organization. Of course, it can be this, but it can also be something as simple as the vision for how you want a conversation to play out, or what success would be at the end of a how a meeting turns out, or a consensus on next steps, or alignment around an idea…

If you're talking about a year from now, then you are now in this moment, looking at the future. Whereas if you're talking about a deliverable or a deadline, you're in project management mode or in execution mode, so the words derive your thinking and behaviour and your conversations. So really, vision can be simple, like thinking about what success will look like before you enter into a conversation or meeting or a project. It's not necessarily a deliverable or a deadline.

Sara nodded, "I can see that. But one thing I've been thinking about since last time: what if the vision isn't very clear? I know some of that comes from things like the Imagine exercise, but other times it just feels like we're not even really sure what the final destination is. Or sometimes the vision is clear, but we seem to be fixing problems all the time. I really value trying to remove obstacles for my team, and I feel as though as soon as I remove one, another pops up. I know we've talked about this before, but it's still a struggle."

"Ah," smiled Melissa. "I totally get that. And even though I encourage you to define what success looks like, or to imagine the end-state you want, it's often not obvious or clearly defined. Instead, think about it directionally rather than a specific destination. And still keep focused on the future as much as you can, even if it's just a few steps ahead of where you are now. Let me offer another perspective that I think will address both of your issues." Melissa went on to tell the story of the whitewater kayaker and mountain biker.

"I really like the metaphor of a whitewater kayaking or mountain biking to really talk about this concept of 'what are you moving towards' instead of 'what problems are you trying to fix'?

"If you've ever been whitewater kayaking or whitewater canoeing, when you first look out over the rapids, you see all kinds of turmoil. You see water going in different directions speeding up, slowing down, jumping over rocks and tree roots, spraying upwards and sideways, logs change trajectories or getting stuck in eddies. It can be a little bit intimidating when you're sitting at the top of the watershed looking at how to get through all that. But if you take a moment to pause and look all the way through the rapids all the way down to where your destination is—perhaps the flat water where the whitewater ends and the river returns to calm—something really interesting happens. You really start to see super clearly a path that the water takes that's relatively smooth, and it has a very, very intentional flow between and through all the different barriers, all the different rocks and all the different things in the way.

"And, of course, there are certain spots along the way where the flow of the water stops or abruptly changes direction because of a big rock or a big log across the path or something else that is just really not very easy to get past. But for the most part, there's a really smooth course or flow that the water takes.

"If you can't see to the final destination, you can still look ahead as much as you can see. This happens the same in mountain biking as well, but let's just keep going with the whitewater kayaker.

"If you get into that rapids and you look ten or fifteen feet in front of you, or a few meters in front of you, you can continue to see the line to follow to make it through all the barriers. And where your eyes look, your body and arms take you, and the kayak will too. So, people who are good at this kind of thing, they constantly look ahead ten, fifteen, maybe twenty feet and they follow the path line of the water through all the rocks, past all the rocks and barriers. Because as they know, if you look at the rocks, you will actually hit them, you'll probably get stuck, maybe even flipped over.

"So if you use this metaphor in leadership, you should have an idea of what your destination is, even if you don't know the exact point you're going to end up down that river, but you have an idea of where you're going. That's 'the what' or the vision that we always talk about. And it's pretty far ahead: maybe it's clear, but sometimes maybe you can't see it yet (maybe it's around a bend in the river in the kayaking metaphor, or it's not super clear yet on the leadership side of things). But you have an idea of where you're going to end up. And for as much as possible, you're looking ahead to see the pathway to get to that destination or at least in the right direction.

"And the barriers, the rocks, the risks, the problems, the things that we often get stuck on, are all there—they'll almost always be there. But every time you look at all these problems, you hit them, you spend too much time with them, you get stuck. What you focus on, what you spend time on, where you put your focus, is where you spend most of your time and effort. And if you mostly look forward in the river, you will actually pass right by many of the problems, many of the barriers, many of the things that you otherwise would get fixated on if you're trying to always fix everything along the way. A lot of time, they become irrelevant if you look ahead and not at the barriers. Of course, there will always be some problems or barriers that you have to stop and pay attention to: like a huge rock you can't go by or a big log that is laying across your path. In those cases, you have to stop and find a way around it or remove it. Those are the true problems you need to focus on. But most of us spend far too much time looking at all the problems along the way and forget to look forward through that smooth waterflow, the path line, to the end.

"Similarly with the mountain biker, if you look at the rocks and the trees and the roots along the way, you're going to hit them. Because your bike goes where your eyes look–try it the next time you're on a bike. Again, if we look ahead, you know ten or fifteen feet, a few metres, you can actually follow the path line through all the barriers. And, of course, just like in the river, there'll be times where there are logs across the path that you have to stop and climb over or go around. In the mountain bike metaphor, it might even be harder to actually see the final destination, the final end-state, but you have an idea of where you're going directionally, you have paths to follow. Keep focusing on the way forward.

"Again, linking this to leadership is the same thing. If you have an idea where you're going directionally, you have a vision of where you want to end up, you have a purpose for why you're doing it, and a bit of a plan even knowing it might change, and you stay forward looking, you won't get derailed by the rocks and problems and barriers along the way.

"And while fixing problems is sometimes necessary, often we spend all this effort removing obstacles and barriers and fixing problems. My experience is that leaders who are always looking ahead for the best flow line, often don't even have to address many of the barriers. It sounds too simple to be true, but I've seen it over and over again. Not to mention that 'fixing' is a very reactive experience."

Sara just sat for a minute taking it all in. "Whoa, I think my mind is blown a bit, to be honest. I never thought about it this way. If I continue with your metaphor, it's so tiring to be hauling those rocks off the path or out of the water all the time. But you're right, we spend so much time looking at the problems, the barriers, the gaps, that we forget to lift our head up and look for the smooth path. Wow. I really hope you're right."

Melissa smiled. "I've seen it work over and over again. And, of course, there will sometimes be legitimate problems to figure out a way around, but there just won't be as many. Just keep looking forward. And this also answers your other question about what about those times when it just isn't that clear where the end of the rapids is, or the end of the path the mountain biker is on. If you have a general idea of the direction you're going and where you're heading (especially if you've done the other exercises we've talked about), keep looking ahead and you will be on the path towards your destination."

"Whew! My head is spinning but in such a good way. And with all the shifts I've made so far, it's really exciting to apply what I've learned. I guess what I'm trying to say is that what was once new information for me to wrap my head is now a complete mindset shift. The way I think about everything is better. Clearer, more focused. The part that really gets me is how complicated I thought this was when we started and now I'm like, 'let's go!' I know what I'm doing and how to do it, and I know where I'm going."

Melissa and Sara wrapped up their session for the day with some commitments and next steps.

CHAPTER 11

Celebrating Wins

"For there is always light, if only we're brave enough to see it.
If only we're brave enough to be it."
— *Amanda Gorman*

Melissa and Sara were meeting for the last of their sessions together to wrap up their work and celebrate Sara's wins. They also would look to the future to see what success looks like for Sara now that she's immersed herself in the coaching and made changes in her day-to-day leadership.

Human behavioural change and likewise leadership growth is subtle and cumulative over time. It's important to reflect on successes–big and small. There will be days, maybe even weeks, that you feel like you're treading water, or even moving backwards. But it's the overall change in trajectory that you're celebrating.

At the beginning of their coaching alliance, Sara was a well-liked, empathetic, and caring people-leader. She was appreciated for her ability to get things done, and she was known as someone who is always ready to jump in and help out others in the organization. She was valued highly by the organization. However, despite her good reputation and reviews, she wasn't seen as strategic enough to move into a VP position.

Melissa and Sara reflected on the successes she's had and where she's made progress in her leadership journey. Together, they looked back on the path she's travelled, acknowledged her growth, and appreciated her wins and successes.

Melissa began the conversation. "We started with you wanting to understand what your boss meant when he said that you're not strategic enough at your last performance review. Now that we've explored this and what it means to be strategic in leadership, I think you have a whole new set of skills and tools and habits to go forward with. **When you reflect back on the last five or six months, what successes have you had?**

Sara immediately was able to express what was different for her since coaching with Melissa. "One of the most important changes is that I've become much more intentional in all my approaches each day, in my decisions and in my preparation—in everything really, instead of just reacting to whatever comes my way. The awareness I built around this has been transformational.

"I set time in my calendar to think about the bigger picture and this really helps to get me away from the minutiae of the day to day. I see now that when I choose the most important things to work on, when I am being intentional instead of reactionary, when I am consciously choosing, my effort goes into what's really important and more gets done."

Melissa asked, "How does it feel?"

"I feel more in control. Less frantic, less stressed, and not pulled in so many directions. I feel confident when I walk into meetings because first of all, I'm not running from something else, completely scattered. I've also put some intentional thinking into the purpose of the meeting, the value I want to contribute, **what would success look like**, and the overall dynamics and goals of what we're there to achieve. Sometimes it takes only a few seconds or minutes to do this, but it makes all the difference."

Melissa nodded, "These are great realizations."

"And," Sara added, "strangely, I feel more energized. I'm not as drained at the end of the day. It's like all these things I'm doing now feel like I'm saying yes to myself more."

Melissa nodded again. "Well, it makes sense. When you're choosing what you spend your time on, your energy flows in the right places, you're more likely to meet your big goals, and you feel accomplished, you know it's helping you evolve into a future you want."

"Yes. I'm definitely being more thoughtful about what kind of future I want and then intentionally doing the things I need to be doing towards it."

"I'm so happy for you, Sara. I don't know if I said it before but it's worth repeating: It's common to become addicted to the adrenaline of old work habits."

When you are used to being looked to as the go-to person, and you're used to the satisfaction of getting things done, it's easy to thrive on the execution part of things. Completing a task, checking things off a to-do list, being seen as the one who saved the day at the last minute, it's easy to keep moving forward with the next thing and the next thing.

Before you know it, you lose track of how it's all adding up. It's like working without an end goal, even though there always is an end goal.

More intentional, conscious thinking leads to more intentional, conscious doing. Scheduling thinking time doesn't mean you lose traction. As you develop this new habit, *thinking* starts to feel more and more like productive time. Instead of constantly *doing*, you build the strategic muscle in leadership. That being said, action is the next step, but it's thoughtful and intentional action.

Melissa turned back to Sara and asked, "Let's talk about your Big Rocks. How are you doing with those?"

"Well, I'm at least getting into the habit of booking time in my calendar for the bigger stuff, so I schedule Imagine time, planning, and creative work, but if I'm to be honest, I don't always stick to it. Even though I schedule it, I still get derailed. But I know it's okay; I don't feel bad that I don't always stick to it. Just seeing it in front of me reminds me of something I'm still working on getting better at. Seeing it there gives me permission to shift time to important things now that later would become urgent. That feels a lot like success to me because I notice my self-talk is very different now. Whereas I always used to default to, 'you have other more urgent things to do now Sara'…now it's there as an important thing for me to prioritize, so I'm getting there!"

"That's a great awareness," Melissa said, then suggested, "Maybe every time you neglect taking time for your Big Rocks, give yourself an opportunity to say yes to them one more time. You mentioned getting derailed sometimes. Let's talk about this a bit more. When you get derailed, what happens?"

Sara reflected, "I'm way, way better now at picking myself up from things that go awry. Icky conversations used to take me forever to bounce back from. Also, when I plan outcomes and unexpected obstacles interfere with my projections, I used to get angry. But I'm better at collecting myself, brushing myself off and moving on."

"That's good," Melissa said, "But now I'm asking you to consider more than getting over it. I'd love for you to remember to ask those strategic questions we've talked so much about:

- **What would success look like?**
- **What the desired future?**
- **What's the big picture?**
- **What trends are we noticing?**
- **What is the connection between X and Y?**
- **What's the impact we want to have?**
- **What's the purpose?**
- **What are the benefits?**
- **A year from now, what will be important?**

Melissa reminded Sara that using strategic questions or even just strategic language also forces you to actually think about these things and also forces others to think about these things. And over the past six months together, Sara has had many examples to choose from to practice formulating and asking strategic questions. There is another way to shift conversations and that's to simply use more strategic language. It's a bit of a trick, but a highly effective exercise is to brainstorm a bunch of strategic words, words like: metaview, future, big picture, six months from now, one year from now, strategic, intentional, plan, vision, roadmap, strategy, integration, synergy, cross-functional, trends, predictions, expectations, interconnection. And whenever you find yourself caught in the tactical, entangled in the details, stuck in problems, focused on *doing*, or just not really focused on being strategic, just use one of these words. It makes *you* think about strategic stuff in that moment, and it also drives strategic conversations with others. If you're talking about the interconnection between two departments, or the trends related to a product design, your thoughts and conversations will naturally start to reflect that strategic conversion. It has the added benefit of also helping others see you as more strategic which helps your overall reputation too.

"That sounds really easy," Sara said.

Melissa went on to remind Sara that when they first met, Sara said she wanted to be known for developing other leaders on her team. She asked Sara how she has grown in this area and what positive changes she's seen.

Sara told Melissa, "I have a new default. I don't jump in to rescue them the minute they come to me with a question. I used to be afraid that if I gave them too much to handle, they would become overwhelmed. Not true. Turns out it empowered them to make more decisions on their own, and they like it.

And the few things that were overwhelming or too much, they just surfaced so much sooner so we could address them head-on instead of everyone just scrambling to get them done and me picking up the slack."

"Tell me some of the ways you respond now. Do you have any examples of what that looks like?"

"Well, I'm responding differently to any request or questions they have. I pause a lot these days. Pausing before answering gives me a minute to think about what I'm about to do or say next. I make sure I'm not just solving their problem for them if I know that with a bit of guidance, they can figure it out. Sometimes I'll ask them good, strategic, 'what' questions to help them apply logic to the problem or get them to define future success and what they're hoping to achieve, which often points to the next step to act on. Even when I do give them more specific advice, I'm quick to follow it up with additional questions to make sure they're taking the idea on as their own and know where to go next with it. Or they decide together on next steps for them to take. Sometimes I even send them back to think it through a bit more or to figure things out a bit more using some of her input or suggestions, but rarely do I take it from them and do it."

Sara paused and then added, "That's a huge change and I can already see some tremendous growth in a few of my people. It's very gratifying."

"And how do you think this has helped you be a leader who develops others?" Melissa asked.

Sara continued excitedly, "I'm already seeing how this change in me is creating change in them. I see so many of my people doing more and gaining confidence in themselves. They're coming to me less often and taking charge of situations and making decisions they would not have made without me before I was coached by you. And now that it's not necessarily easier or quicker for them to ask me or to have me do it, they really only come to me for things that really do need my oversight."

Melissa smiled. "Sara, you are definitely stepping into more of the leader they really need rather than just the one that is convenient in that moment."

Sara's old way of doing things didn't feed their progress. By giving them more space to explore and experiment with their own capabilities, they can experience more successes, they are more autonomous. They are also taking more initiative on things because of their increased confidence and independence. Sara knows that even though her past intentions were good, she has found a better way forward. And they both acknowledge that Sara is now spending more of her time on the business and on strategic issues that help her team and division be more successful and integrate more with organizational needs.

Melissa wondered, **"What's another major insight, or discovery so far?"**

"To answer this, I'd have to say there are two key areas where what I do now has drastically transformed how I do things." Sara went on to explain: "The first area, without a doubt, is the way I communicate and present at meetings. I feel the biggest lift in my confidence in my formal presentations, but also even when I'm speaking to my team, or when I speak up more ad-hoc in the senior leadership meetings. I prepare for all these things differently. My presentations are more focused and more aligned with what they care about–what helps them run the business better. It makes so much sense and has made all the difference because now, the way I present is being noticed and applauded. I laugh now at how few slides I come with and to be honest, I know they love it because they're actually with me and fidgeting less. I'm observing more, noting what they talk about, listening without preparing my answer, and so I hit the mark more often. I feel more connected and am more comfortable contributing. This required next level thinking that never even entered my mind before. I think a lot more about the audience and what they care about–whether that's something formal or not. I did that before, of course, I'm just doing it better."

Melissa thought for a minute and then asked Sara, "Aside from presentations, if I asked for some other specific ways that you're communicating more or differently, could you name a few?"

"Well, I'm really observing and listening to my boss' boss in meetings and am noticing what catches her attention, what she lingers on, and what she makes statements about. Also, I took a giant leap—at least it was for me—and about a month ago, I asked my boss' boss if it would be appropriate for me to sit in on a certain strategic meeting that I'd not been invited to in the past.

"Another way that I'm communicating differently is something else I want to celebrate. I'm completely different in how I lead planning meetings with my team. My more strategic understanding of vision versus goals/outcomes has completely changed how I approach these meetings. I make sure we all feel safe contributing our big ideas. My approach is completely different now. I ask them if-you-could-do-anything questions, as if there were no limits, and I encourage them to imagine the wild and crazy and seemingly impossible and ask them to throw it all out there. I use the first few minutes to remind everyone that no idea is too big, too loud, too crazy, or too impossible not to be brought to the table and then I make sure to provide a space that feels safe to have fun. Of course, we do look at how this might integrate into our real world at a later time, but there is so much more innovation and creativity and honestly more bold ideas of what we could be doing, or at least what we want to influence and impact in our products, in our organization and in the broader world. Sometimes it's small stuff, which is totally great too. And sometimes it's bolder than we've ever been before. There's still a bit of hesitancy, but I see that shifting slowly. Honestly, it's so exciting and inspiring."

"I really appreciate you sharing this with me," Melissa said. "And I love that you're able to bring this to your team. Most people are afraid to think beyond what they think is possible or practical, so they keep it small. By providing this space you're giving everyone permission to express their creativity, to be aspirational and maybe even a bit bold. The practical side comes out in the actions, but the actions are driving to something better.

"We've spoken a few times about your peer relationships and how important those are for strategic leadership, but also for having the influence you want in an organization. What has changed on that side?" Melissa asked.

Sara answered, "I'm definitely doing better, but I still want to pay more attention to setting up time to meet with peers that I don't normally meet with, you know, to bring myself into the wider dynamics of the organization. There's so much that goes on around me that I don't know much about. I do meet with my peers when it relates to initiatives I'm spearheading, or if they request a meeting, of course, but I want to be more intentional about broadening my network across the business, and developing the relationships I already have. And I want to change the conversations so they're more strategic. I'd like to know more about what my peers are into and the trends they're seeing. **What are their challenges**? I just always felt too busy before. Now I understand that not only is this not wasted time, but in fact, it's essential to bring me a wider and more clear perspective of the whole organization—and to give them the same. I get the importance of it, so I will do more of this. I also want to spend more time with my peers talking about the senior executive team, the board, our customers, our stakeholders, and probably even sometimes our staff. I'm realizing that they have leadership contributions to make and that they could benefit from my perspective too. We can accomplish so much more together when we're integrated and aligned and supporting each other."

"This is great, Sara." Melissa added, "Relationships with peers typically increases your ability to influence and helps develop allies outside your areas of business. The insight that you gain into other areas of the business is invaluable. Doing more of this allows you to make better decisions, create better visions and strategies and plans. It broadens your perspective, makes your own work more meaningful, more integrated, and more connected to a bigger—often shared—purpose."

"It's totally worth the extra effort and time it takes to connect with my peers across the organization," Sara agreed. "I can see many advantages and no reason not to keep it up."

"You know, Sara, some of the changes you've made might feel like small things, but from where I sit, they look a lot like significant successes. You know at a deeper level that successes are not always only the end results. It's also how you go about your day-to-day and how you interact with others. You've come so far with all of this."

"True, I guess," Sara agreed. "Remember the Leadership Action Plan I did way back when we started? Well, I've been using it all along, but I recently rescored myself to see how I'm doing. I originally scored a 5.5 out of 10 for myself and before coming into this last session, I was curious so I redid it and scored an 7.5. And I think I raised the bar on 'what would success look like?' so that growth is likely even higher than it seems with the scoring. I have higher expectations for myself now. But not in a burdensome way—more in a stimulating and motivating way. It's like I was so busy doing so much before, that I didn't allow myself to have these bigger desires. I look forward to coming to work in ways I haven't in years. I liked my job before, but now I just can't wait to see what else is possible for the team, the organization, our products, and frankly myself.

"Huge kudos. That's quite a lot to celebrate," Melissa said. "So, what excites you going forward?"

Sara answered, "Honestly, it's the passion project I mentioned before. When I ask myself your favourite question, **what does success look like to me down the road**, the answer is always to bring this project to life. I want it seen, heard, and accepted, and now I know how to get there. This really, really energizes me, Melissa. I know what I need to do, and I've started. At last, it doesn't feel impossible anymore. In fact, it's come alive in me. I've made it a priority and every week I'm doing something towards it. I think about it, plan it out, research it, talk about it with others, and will be putting a business case together. I'm envisioning the end state. I know what actions I can take over time to bring it in closer, make it more real and I'm doing it!"

Melissa gave her a big smile. "Well, I'm excited for you too! It really goes to show that if every day we choose the important things, everything that's truly important gets done. Everything you do towards your vision adds up."

Sara nodded in agreement. "And the best part of it is that instead of it feeling like I'm stealing time and focus away from other important things, it feels as though everything that needs to get done is getting done."

"Instead of playing catch up, which seems to be a growing trend in a lot of people's workdays, you're able to focus on the desired outcomes more," Melissa commented. "It's like developing new skin around accomplishing more. The day-to-day stuff gets done without always being one thing to do. Before we go, **what else can we celebrate that's changed since working together?"**

"Well," Sara reflected, "generally speaking, I learned a lot about myself—things I never thought about before or just assumed I knew. Through the course of working with you, Melissa, I realize that I wasn't adventurous. I approached my work the way I always did. It's as if my role as a leader grew and demanded more of me but I wasn't growing with it. Almost like, 'this has always worked for me and my team before, so why change anything?' I think I was getting stale.

"I see now that it's a good thing to venture out of old patterns and try new ways of doing things. You've especially highlighted for me how important it is to bring awareness into what I do and why. By journaling, thinking, consciousness, questioning, wondering, imagining…I've become clearer, more future-focused and definitely more strategic. I can say with confidence that I am a better leader today than I was when we started, and I want to thank you for showing me what I'm capable of."

"Oh, you're welcome. It's what I'm here to do. I can see that growth in you over just these several weeks. Keep at it. Take what works for you and keep putting it into practice." Then Melissa shifted the conversation to the future. "So tell me, Sara, when you think about next year, maybe even your next performance review, **what does success look like for you?**"

Sara's answer was immediate. "Oh my gosh. In the short term I have to say it's to get a performance review that doesn't reiterate that I'm not strategic enough. Of course, if there's a VP position that's right for me in the coming year and I get it that would be huge.

"I also want to say that what I've done here with you has created a shift that has transformed my leadership abilities forever. You gave me a new and expanded way of thinking of myself as a leader, especially in relation to others: to my team, my peers, my higher ups and even beyond my sector. I understand better how we are all pieces of a machine; when I am being strategic, I am contributing beyond what I would call limited thinking. I only knew what I knew and functioned from that space. I have an expanded awareness that allows me to see beyond those limitations. Thanks to you, Melissa, I feel much more capable and confident in the contributions that I can make now. I'm grateful to you for what you've shown me and how I've been able to grow right from the beginning."

Melissa applauded her. "You did this, Sara. You got yourself to this point, not me. You've allowed yourself to open your mind to some new ideas, new courses of action and alternate views. I've enjoyed watching you try things, accustom yourself to the ideas we've talked about. Not only are you recognized for your role as a key member of the organization's team, but now everyone will see that you are also a strategic leader. I don't think you'll be hearing 'not strategic enough' at your next review."

Sara chuckled, "Ha-ha—no, I don't think so."

"Just continue to be intentional," Melissa cautioned, "because as we all know, the road isn't always smooth or predictable." These new habits are starting to be ingrained, and they will continue to need attention because the fires and derailers and tasks lists and emails and deadlines will continue to call your attention."

And then it was time for Melissa to say goodbye to Sara.

***

If I could speak directly to the readers who have made it this far in the book and have generously decided to spend time with what I offer within these pages, I would love to say: when you close the cover and go back to your life, spend some time intentionally thinking about this:

"What does success look like a year from now—and what do you have to do to get there?"

To you and your wins,

Melissa

ABOUT THE AUTHOR

Melissa Creede helps leaders to stop leading from their inboxes, and to start leading from their strategic goals and vision instead.

She believes that good leaders focus on what's important, and not necessarily on what's urgent. A former business executive, Melissa believes in the power of collective action to lead the way for a future that is defined by compassion, equity, and harmony.

As an executive leadership coach, Melissa's sweet spot is to coach leaders committed to making a positive difference in the world, particularly on important social causes.

www.ingramcontent.com/pod-product-compliance
Lightning Source LLC
Chambersburg PA
CBHW071145120626
46546CB00006B/2137